CRUSADE FOR DEMOCRACY

CRUSADE FOR DEMOCRACY

Progressive Education at the Crossroads

Revised Edition

Daniel Tanner

Published by State University of New York Press, Albany

For information, contact State University of New York Press, Albany, NY
www.sunypress.edu

Production, Jenn Bennett
Marketing, Michael Campochiaro

Library of Congress Cataloging-in-Publication Data

Tanner, Daniel.
  Crusade for democracy : progressive education at the crossroads / Daniel Tanner. — Rev. ed.
    pages   cm
  Includes bibliographical references and index.
  ISBN 978-1-4384-5646-1 (pbk. : alk. paper) — ISBN 978-1-4384-5645-4 (hardcover : alk. paper) — ISBN 978-1-4384-5647-8 (e-book) 1. John Dewey Society—History. 2. Progressive education—United States. I. John Dewey Society. II. Title.
  L13.J64T36 2015
  370.1—dc23

                                            2014027110

10 9 8 7 6 5 4 3 2 1

A publication of the
John Dewey Society for the Study of Education and Culture
in commemoration of the eightieth anniversary of founding

In tribute to

Henry Harap
Jesse H. Newlon
Paul R. Hanna
William H. Kilpatrick
and
of course
Laurel

History deals with the past,
but this past is the history of the present.
—John Dewey

CONTENTS

PREFACE TO THE REVISED EDITION

This new edition is not only an update of the original edition, but a reevaluation of the prospects of the John Dewey Society in the perspective of its eventful and courageous history.

Founded during the disastrous years of the Great Depression, the history of the John Dewey Society reveals how the Society managed to embrace social action with the advancement of scholarship in the defense of American democracy. The Society gained some notable victories, such as in the battle for academic freedom in the public schools and higher education. But even when the Dewey Society lost out in a particular struggle, it always was on the right side of history.

The Great Depression gave rise to some of the most experimental efforts in American education—such as the Eight-Year Study, sponsored by the Progressive Education Association; *The Social Frontier*—a journal addressed to teachers in examining the most pervasive social issues and problems of the times; and the *Building America* series of paperback books, sponsored by the Society for Curriculum Study, which engaged adolescents in the uses of documentary materials for investigating the problems of democracy.

The Society for Curriculum Study, which became the Association for Supervision and Curriculum Development (ASCD), was founded by the very same individuals who founded the John Dewey Society.

Although the John Dewey Society lost out in its struggle to save the Progressive Education Association and its journal and failed to save *The Social Frontier* and *Building America* for want of the needed financial resources, the Society itself not only managed to survive, but gained great respect through these action engagements and scholarly publications. From the Great Depression through the Cold War years, the Society published sixteen yearbooks which addressed the most vital educational issues and problems.

However, during the past decade or so, as chronicled in these pages, the John Dewey Society sharply reduced its publications program and discontinued its programs of social action as conceived by its founders. Unfortunately, even in terms of scholarship, its publications program consisted mainly of its journal, *Education and Culture*, which was focused on educational theory. The vital connection of the Dewey Society with school and society and with child and curriculum was no longer apparent even in the critical times of assault on the public schools and the drive to split up the American public school system with charter schools. The John Dewey Lecture of 2014 appeared to be an exception in addressing these issues, but unfortunately the publication of the Annual Lecture had been discontinued after 2006.

The closing pages of this book include excerpts from John Dewey's last published statement just before his death. The statement is from the Introduction to a book sponsored by the John Dewey Society. The statement addresses the problem of facing the organized attacks on the public schools which, in Dewey's words, "have become more extensive and virulent than ever before."

The statement is especially significant and appropriate because the John Dewey Society was established in the wake of unprecedented attacks on the public schools. From the start, the Society took action to defend the public schools and advance their mission for a free society. John Dewey's statement could well have been written today. The question is whether the John Dewey Society is ready and willing to respond as it did in Dewey's day. In his last published statement, Dewey takes stock of the progressive education movement—its successes and failures over his lifetime—and ends by expressing how educational practice must be transformed into a cooperative transaction of inquiry required for the creation of a democratic society.

The key question raised in the concluding pages of this history of the John Dewey Society is whether the Society can reclaim its legacy. Surely the contemporary social and education conditions augur for the Society, in the words of John Dewey, "to make a new beginning afresh."

Finally, I want to express my appreciation to the research staff of the Alexander Library of Rutgers University for their assistance in providing documents essential for this project, and again to the Rutgers Research Council for the initial grant for the first edition. I am also grateful to Tatyana Podstrelova for her careful work in the word processing of the manuscript.

Daniel Tanner

FOREWORD TO THE FIRST EDITION

What is remarkable about the John Dewey Society is that it still exists. In 1934–35, a group of excited, idealistic young men, at once appalled by the crises of the time and exhilarated by the thought that they might themselves contribute to a large-scale shift in public attitudes and political practices, gathered around the name of the man they considered the greatest educational thinker of the century, and fastened their hopes on that part of his thinking that proclaimed a social mission for the schools.

At about the same time, other groups also formed, with similar goals and a similar sense of mission. Among them were the Progressive Education Association, the Social Frontier Movement, and the publishers of *Building America*. There was a considerable overlap among these groups. They addressed the vital social issues of the times, but they were weak organizationally. They linked themselves with the strong liberal politics of the time and thus gained the approval as well as the enmity of influential figures in the press, on the radio, and in politics. The groups agreed in general on doctrine—indeed, they seemed to some to be doctrinaire. However, they suffered from internal

differences, and they had no agreed-upon agenda. The
Social Frontier group fell prey to its internal tensions; its
publication ceased within a few years, and its members
(except for those on the Teachers College faculty) scattered.
The Progressive Education Association had lost its vitality by the end of World War II, and disappeared for lack
of membership and support early in the fifties. *Building
America* disappeared without a trace after it was attacked
by the resurgent political Right in California at the end of
World War II.

It is interesting that none of these groups had a clearcut program to suggest for the amelioration of the problems of the day. They tried to live on their own elan.
Those organizations that survived had changed with the
times. They admitted into their number people who did
not wholly subscribe to their doctrines, and they took on
practical service activities. The Association for Supervision
and Curriculum Development is a good example. Begun
early in the forties by uniting the Society for Curriculum
Study (a group begun by Henry Harap, one of the two or
three organizers of the John Dewey Society) and the field-
oriented NEA Department of Supervisors and Directors of
Instruction, ASCD has thrived. Now a field-service organization, it has a huge membership, but its early commitment toward progressive doctrine has disappeared.

All of these organizations had to survive their early
growing pains, and none had a more difficult struggle
than the John Dewey Society. It is remarkable that the
John Dewey Society did not perish from internal bicker-
ing like the others. It did not, as Daniel Tanner's research
makes clear, because from the beginning it tolerated differences in point of view. While Harap and the others wanted
only "genuine liberals" in 1935, the sixty-odd founding

members differed in outlook, yet respected one another, and no struggle for power took place. As the political and intellectual climate changed with the onset of World War II and the postwar years, so did the content of the JDS meetings and publications. The tolerance of differing points of view in the John Dewey Society allowed a much more heterogeneous group of successors to assume leadership in the Society.

The John Dewey Society survived at least three major crises—crises like those that led to the destruction of the Society's contemporary reform organization. The first of these, as Daniel Tanner's research indicates, was the sharp disagreement between the group around Ohio State University and those at Teachers College over the tone and content of George Counts' well-known *Dare the School Build a New Social Order?* That pamphlet seemed doctrinaire, and therefore undemocratic, to the Ohio State group and some others. But the quarrel never came to a head, though everyone knew it existed. The differences were tolerated.

A second crisis arose at the time of the suspension of the John Dewey Society yearbooks. Those books had accounted for much of the Society's national reputation, and some members of the Society thought that with the suspension of the yearbooks the Society had lost its meaning. It had not, as it turned out; again, the group managed to make a change that matched the times.

Another crisis arose when the Society tried, and failed, to save the Progressive Education Association, and earlier, the *Building America* series. It may be that those were the most severe of the crises. The John Dewey Society, in efforts to preserve the PEA and *Building America*, was trying to be true to its origins by continuing the traditional debates of the thirties. But twenty years had passed; the nation had survived the Great Depression and World War II. The struggle to keep the dialectic of the 1930s alive could have destroyed the John Dewey Society, but the Society proved flexible enough to change with the times.

If the founders of the Society were still with us and active, some of them would lament the loss of these battles, and would consider the Society to have been untrue to its purpose, which they saw as saving the country for democracy and, in particular, preventing the political Right from damaging the fabric of American society.

The alternative view is that the Society was truer to the ideas of John Dewey than its founders understood. Dewey especially, consistently questioned the given. There is a lesson to be learned from the survival of the John Dewey Society, despite its early hard times. The lesson is to be found in that part of Dewey's message to us that calls the given into question, whatever the given is—including Dewey's own political beliefs of the first half of the twentieth century. If the principal function of education is to make the given problematic, then the John Dewey Society has survived because of the heterogeneity of its founders and of the inheritors of their vision.

The Society has consistently examined the relationship between education and culture. The early yearbooks of the Society dealt with flaws in the culture, and therefore with the mission of education to remedy such flaws. The Society's yearbooks proceeded to examine the flaws in the institutions of education, and to propose improvements. More recently, the John Dewey Lectures, now published by the Teachers College Press, have examined the culture as it has evolved during the half century since the Society's founding. Always, the Society's activities call the given into question. The Society, true to Dewey's spirit, asks the present to defend itself. In so doing, it remains contemporary. Many say that these times are a question mark. The John Dewey Society is one of the questioners.

Arthur W. Foshay, President
John Dewey Society, 1988–1989

PREFACE TO THE FIRST EDITION

As we entered the closing decade of our century, global events gave renewed recognition to democracy as a living ideal. The concept of democracy not only signaled a momentous turning point in global political affairs, but gave Americans cause for reexamining the American political and educational experience.

From the mid-1960s through the late 1980s, radical revisionists, critical theorists and neo-Marxists had portrayed the American public schools and Dewey's experimentalism in an adverse light while failing to acknowledge the contributions of those who fought to uphold and promote the democratic-liberal traditions in popular education in the face of great opposition. The topic of democracy, which had been so pervasive in our educational literature over the first half of the twentieth century, seemed to become unfashionable. Now, global events have brought the word *democracy* to the front pages of our newspapers while the professional literature in education reveals that *democracy* has again become a topic of great educational significance.

This book tells the story of a small group of American educators who fought to advance democratic educational

principles and practices over a period spanning three critical eras of our modern history—from the disastrous years
of the Great Depression through the great conflict of World
War II, and through the cold war years of McCarthyism
and a divided world.

The small group of educators who are the focus of this
story were founding members of the John Dewey Society for the Study of Education and Culture. Although the
story relates to the origins and activities of the Society,
it extends into the life and times of a group of educators
who worked from the conviction that the struggle for the
survival and growth of American democracy could not be
conducted apart from the public schools. Theirs was not a
naive conviction, for they recognized that the problems of
public education (e.g., educational opportunity) are inter-
connected with our social, political, economic, and cultural
problems. They sought to connect the school curriculum
to the pervasive social problems and issues of the times.
They fought against infringements on academic freedom
from the extreme Right and against those on the political
Left who contended that the schools be made the instruments to "build a new social order." They fought for open
inquiry in the curriculum and against indoctrination in any
form. They were key figures in upholding and advancing
the American democratic-liberal tradition.

Many of the events documented in this story are little
known or have gone unrecognized in much of our literature in educational history-for example, the role of the
John Dewey Society in assuming publication of *The Social
Frontier* and later *Progressive Education* while seeking to
find permanent sponsorship for these journals at a time of
economic hardship and ideological attack; the failed efforts
of the Society's Executive Board to save the Progressive

Education Association; the efforts of the Society in upholding academic freedom in our schools and colleges during times when such freedom was never more severely tested; the exciting yearbooks of the Society, published over a quarter of a century, examining the most pervasive problems of American democracy; and the fact that John Dewey's last published piece of writing was done at the invitation of the John Dewey Society, in which he pointed out that the progressive education movement should be seen as part of the wider social movement for the improvement of the human condition.

This is the story of how a small group of educators from widely varied areas of specialism in the field of education joined together with visionary school leaders to address the threats to the democratic-liberal tradition in school and society. These educators realized that the deepest and widest philosophical questions relating to the democratic prospect were not in the province of philosophers talking among themselves, but vital concerns of school people and the public at large. The story is one of shared vision and optimism in the face of continued setbacks. The legacy to be learned from the efforts of these educators is that democracy once discovered can never be undiscovered.

I am greatly indebted to Glen Hass, Arthur W. Foshay, and Jonas F. Soltis—who served as succeeding Presidents of the John Dewey Society during the course of this project, and to their governing boards, for their support. I am also indebted to the Rutgers University Research Council for a grant to help get this project under way.

For their critical readings of the manuscript and constructive suggestions, I owe a scholarly debt to Arthur Brown, Arthur W. Foshay, William H. Schubert, Philip L. Smith, and Jonas F. Soltis.

I am grateful to Donald P. Cottrell, Ralph W. Tyler, and the late Sidney Hook who submitted written statements of their recollections of the early years of the John Dewey Society. Ralph Tyler also gave generously of his time for interviews.

Sheila Ryan, Curator of Manuscripts in Special Collections of the Morris Library at Southern Illinois University, supplied me with copies of the minutes of some of the early meetings of the Board of Directors of the John Dewey Society, along with copies of letters, memos, and other records of the Society's early activities. Her assistance was indeed essential to this project.

Appreciation is extended to William Van Til, a former President of the John Dewey Society, who also provided me with copies of earlier records of the Society. Special thanks go to Robert C. Morris, Secretary of the John Dewey Society, for his suggestions on obtaining certain records and for his cooperation and support.

Finally, I thank my colleague Martin Kling for his interest and support of this project, and Marion Ann Keller for typing the manuscript.

Daniel Tanner

INTRODUCTION TO THE FIRST EDITION

As president of the John Dewey Society in its fifty-fifth year, I am especially pleased to have the honor to write a few words of introduction to Dan Tanner's very readable history of this remarkable organization.

Dewey believed in the power of human intelligence to deal with the deepest and most crucial social and educational problems that inevitably arise in a world of change. He believed that social intelligence was best utilized in the open climate of a democratic society. In fact, fostering democratic association was one of the key purposes of education for Dewey.

The founders of the John Dewey Society for the Study of Education and Culture were educators. The mission of the Society as they defined it was to promote scholarly and scientific investigations of problems pertaining to the place and function of education in social change. In the spirit of John Dewey, this was to be done not from some doctrinaire philosophical position, but rather from an arena of open dialogue, debate, and decision making in a democratic setting.

Through its sponsorship of yearbooks, the annual John Dewey Lecture, and special-interest group programs at

AERA (American Educational Research Association) meetings, members and friends of the John Dewey Society have kept the spirit of Deweyan inquiry alive for fifty five years. In this history of its founding, Tanner traces its efforts from the troubled times of its beginning in the Great Depression, through the threatening post-World War II years of McCarthyism, to the present era of reform in American education and the democratization of societies all over the world.

This is a history of voluntary association, a group of committed people who have put their trust in the power of human intelligence and education to address the most pressing issues faced by an evolving democratic society.

Social, educational, and intellectual historians interested in the progressive era will find Tanner's research rich, insightful, and illuminating, and every reader will find his story fascinating and engrossing.

Jonas F. Soltis
President, The John Dewey Society, 1990–1991

I

ON THE BRINK OF DISASTER

We were in the midst of a frightful depression. Many
people thought that we were on the brink of an economic disaster.

On January 3, 1934, Henry Harap of Western Reserve University wrote to his friend Paul Hanna of Teachers College
asking him to persuade Jesse Newlon (also of Teachers
College) to convene a meeting of liberal colleagues in education during the annual conference of the Department of
Superintendence of the National Education Association,
scheduled to be held in Cleveland in February of that year.
Appalled by the frightful conditions of the Great Depression, Harap recognized that while educational liberals
were deeply concerned with the national emergency and
the significance of the public schools in helping to rebuild
the nation, they had not explicated any clear ideas as to
the actual role that the schools should serve in that effort.
From this modest beginning, the seed was sown for what
was to become the John Dewey Society for the Study of
Education and Culture.

At the age of forty-one, Henry Harap was then Associate Professor of Education at Western Reserve University
in Cleveland where he was gaining national recognition as
a leader in the emerging field of curriculum development.
Harap had immigrated to the United States from Austria

in 1900 at age seven with his parents. It was a time when the immigration from Europe was reaching its peak. "No such great movement of peoples was ever known before in history," wrote Ellwood P. Cubberley (1947, p. 482). Harap was a product of the New York City Public Schools, and had gone on to earn his bachelor's degree at the City College of New York, and his M.A. and Ph.D. from Teachers College, Columbia. He taught briefly in public and private schools in New York City. Following his tenure at Western Reserve, he joined the faculty at Ohio State for the 1936–1937 academic year, and then went on to George Peabody College until his retirement in 1959.

Paul Hanna was born in Iowa in 1902, earned his bachelor's degree at Hamline, and his M.A. and Ph.D. at Teachers College. He had served as superintendent of schools in West Winfield, New York, from 1925 through 1927. At the time he received Henry Harap's letter, Hanna was Assistant Professor at Teachers College and a research associate of Jesse Newlon at the Lincoln School. He joined the faculty in education at Stanford University in 1935 where he became the Lee J. Jacks Professor in 1954. Following his retirement from Stanford, Hanna served as a senior research fellow at the Hoover Institution on War, Revolution, and Peace until his death in 1988. A leading figure in the field of social studies curriculum and international education, Hanna chaired the editorial board of the *Building America* series of monthly paperback texts from 1935 to 1948. The texts were widely used in social studies classes in the junior and senior high schools, reaching a circulation of over a million copies an issue. The *Building America* series had originated as a project of the Society for Curriculum Study when Henry Harap was serving as chair of the Society's Executive Committee. *Building America* was conceived to enable youngsters to examine the nation's pervasive social problems critically and constructively. However, during the early years of the Cold War, the series became a victim of attack by the conservative press, the ultraright, and the California Joint Legislative Fact-Finding Committee on Un-American Activities. The last issue appeared at the end of 1948 when school boards were having the texts destroyed.

Jesse Newlon served on the Editorial Board of *Building America* from 1936 through 1942. He had been brought to Teachers College in 1927 to direct the Lincoln School following a career of creative curriculum leadership as Superintendent of Schools in Denver. In Denver, Newlon had supported the work of teachers in curriculum development with released time, funding, and consultation. The *Denver Research Monograph Series* contained the results of these efforts and the issues of this publication were in demand by school systems throughout the United States and abroad. Born in Indiana in 1882, Newlon earned his bachelor's degree at Indiana University in 1907. He went on to serve as a teacher and principal in the schools of Indiana and Illinois, and as principal and later Superintendent of Schools in Lincoln Nebraska before going on to Denver. He earned his master's at Teachers College in 1914 and an LL.D. at the University of Denver in 1922. Newlon became director of the program in educational foundations at Teachers College in 1938.

Looking back to the conditions of the Great Depression when Henry Harap wrote to Paul Hanna, Harap recalled that "It was a time of a terrific awakening of the schools to their educational responsibilities" (1970, p. 157). Harap's comment can in no way be taken to mean that the Great Depression was a propitious event for educators and the schools. The "tremendous reawakening" was marked by great disputation among educators of that day and great opposition by business interests to progressive educational reform. As Harap recalled, "We were in the midst of a frightful depression. Many people thought that we were on the brink of an economic disaster" (p. 157). In his letter to Jesse Newlon on April 27, 1934, Harap wrote, "The movement to the right has definitely crystallized. The newly invigorated, dominant economic groups are more defiant than they have been in five years."

No chronicle of the perverse social and economic conditions of that period in our history can possibly convey the despair and suffering which were so rampant. In looking back on any historic period, there is the popular cliché, "Those were simpler times." However, life was not so simple under conditions of unprecedented economic and social dislocation. Unemployment had reached epidemic proportions.

The New Deal reforms of relief, child welfare, social security, unemployment insurance, federal work projects for the unemployed, rural electrification, minimum wages, agricultural reconstruction, and so on, were yet to be put into concerted action. The storm clouds of Nazism and Fascism were hovering over Europe. Amenities that are taken for granted today were unavailable—from refrigeration in the home to antibiotics in medicine. Extensive areas of rural America were still without electricity. Under the menacing conditions of the Great Depression, many knowledgeable people believed that the American economy could not possibly survive.

It was under these conditions that Henry Harap was impelled to write his letter to Paul Hanna. The response was prompt and affirmative. In an exchange of correspondence,

Harap and Newlon compiled a list of potential participants for the meeting of liberal-minded educators in early February of 1934. Letters were sent to forty-two educators inviting them to attend a luncheon meeting at the Hollenden Hotel in Cleveland on Sunday, February 25, 1934. Only five replied that they would be unable to attend.

II

THE FORMATIVE MEETINGS

"For the first time, the general social point of view in education which we share was vigorously presented and got an adequate hearing."

Henry Harap was to recount twenty-one years later, from his notes, what he considered to be some of the possible activities of the proposed organization as seen by "a liberal educator in the hinterland of Cleveland." These activities included a program for the public schools, a bulletin on educational and economic reform, contacts with liberal organizations outside public education, defense of educators against unwarranted attacks by special-interest groups, protection of academic freedom of teachers and school administrators, and the support of liberal ideas in educational organizations in which such views are ordinarily ignored (p. 158).

Harap recalled that the discussion at the meeting on February 25, 1934 was "vigorous and exciting" with the participants being "strong-minded independent thinkers who talked frankly and vehemently about their social and economic views." A second session was held on Tuesday evening, February 27, 1934. Harap reported that "No single economic or educational theory was accepted as the official position of the whole group." The group elected Harold Rugg to serve as secretary pro tem.

A follow-up meeting was held on October 6 and 7, 1934 in New York City at the Hotel Pennsylvania with some thirty members of the original group in attendance. The letter of invitation to this meeting was signed by Harold Rugg and Jesse Newlon. On February 6 of the following year, a letter signed by George Counts, Jesse Newlon, and Harold Rugg invited all who had attended any of the earlier meetings to participate in a conference at the Annual Meeting of the NEA's Department of Superintendence at the Hotel Traymore in Atlantic City on February 24. The letter stated that, "At this meeting critical issues now confronting education will be considered and definite steps will be taken to launch a strong national society for the scientific study of school and society" (Harap, p. 161).

Harap was to recall that although the letter dated February 6, 1935 signed by George S. Counts, Jesse Newlon, and Harold Rugg identified sixty founding members, the letter acknowledged that, "There is a remote possibility that some names have been omitted from the list." Harap pointed out that R. B. Raup and Ralph Spence of Teachers College should have been on the list, and he stated that "the possibility exists that other names were omitted also" (1970, p. 102). Minutes of the meeting of the Society dated February 23, 1935, obtained from the John Dewey Archives at Southern Illinois University, include a list of sixty-seven persons who attended or who were invited to attend the meeting in Atlantic City. In addition to Raup and Spence, the surname of Bristol appears and is identified as Assistant Superintendent of Schools, Oakland, California. Others listed in the minutes of February 23, 1935 but not included on the list compiled by Counts, Newlon, and Rugg are William D. Boutwell of *School Life*, Maurice Robinson of *Scholastic Magazine*, James M. Shields of Alexandria, Virginia, I. Keith Tyler of Ohio State University, and Carleton Washburne of the Winnetka, Illinois public schools. The minutes state that "All persons whose names appear above were voted in as charter fellows of the new society." The minutes of February 23, 1935 report that the nominating committee had recommended the following members to serve on the first Executive Board of the Society: Hollis L. Caswell of George Peabody College, H. Gordon Hullfish of the Dalton School and Ohio State University, Frank E. Baker of Milwaukee State Teachers College, Jesse Newlon and Harold O. Rugg of Teachers College, and Willard Beatty, Superintendent of the Bronxville, N.Y. public schools. Beatty withdrew and was replaced by Robert Speer of New York University. Rugg also withdrew and was replaced by William Kilpatrick. George S. Counts was added to the Board.

Nevertheless, the organization was still without a name. A year was to pass before the announcement was made that the organization had been formally named the John Dewey Society.

The minutes of the meeting of February 23, 1935 reveal that a committee was assigned to "work over the constitution and present a new constitution at a meeting to be held during the Department of Superintendence (NEA) meeting in 1936." The original constitution bore a temporary name for the organization as "a Society for the Study of Education in its Social Relationships." Annual dues were set at $2.50 for members and $3.50 for fellows (members who were to make a significant contribution to a yearbook or other investigation sponsored by the Society).

At a second meeting of the Executive Board on February 23, 1935, William Kilpatrick was named President of the Board. George D. Stoddard of the University of Iowa replaced Robert Speer on the Board, and Speer was named Secretary of the Board. The Board named John Dewey and the historian Charles Beard as the first outside fellows of the new society. Others named as fellows at the first meeting of the Board were Lewis Mumford, George Coe, Brodus Mitchell, Harold Groves, Merle Curti, Henry P. Fairchild, Boyd H. Bode, Max Otto, W. F. Ogburn, and Paul Douglas.

A list of the founding members of the John Dewey Society is included in the appendix. Serious students of education will instantly recognize most of the names and will take note of the high proportion of young men who were to go on to make vivid and lasting contributions to the advancement of the democratic ideal for American education.

In reviewing the list of founding members, one is also struck by the broad representation of the group from fields other than the social and philosophical foundations of education. The absence of women is apparent. In the exchange of correspondence between Jesse Newlon and Henry Harap in 1934 concerning the compilation of the list of the original group, Newlon raised the question of including women and indicated that he was without prejudice. It was decided to leave the matter to the first meeting of the initial group (Newlon to Harap, January 19, 1934; Harap to Newlon, January 22, 1934; as cited by Johnson, 1977, p. 69).

Soon after the official launching of the Society, women figured prominently in the Society. For example, Hilda Taba and Laura Zirbes of Ohio State served as members of the committee which produced the first yearbook of the John Dewey Society, issued in 1937 under the title, *The Teacher and Society*. (A complete list of the yearbooks and their editors is presented at the end of this publication.)

Harap recalled that Jesse Newlon commented that the setting for the Atlantic City meeting of the formative group on February 24, 1935 was the most significant convention that Newlon had ever attended. "For the first time," said Newlon, "the general social point of view in education which we share was vigorously presented and got an adequate hearing" (p. 161). The outcome of the meeting of February 24, 1935, as reported in *The Social Frontier*, was to organize a society dedicated to the scholarly investigation of the relations of school and society, particularly to the function of education in the process of social change" (April, 1935, p. 3). As Harap related:

> The founders gathered at a breakfast meeting in Atlantic City on Sunday morning, February 24, 1935. The outcome of the conference was to organize a society to "encourage in every way possible and . . . itself conduct scholarly and scientific investigations of the relations of school and society, with particular reference to the place and function of education in the process of social change.
>
> This decision marked the achievement of a goal conceived by a small group of educational liberals who had come together exactly a year earlier to the day. Although the new society had not yet been named, it was informally called the John Dewey group." (1970, p. 162)

SEARCHING FOR A NAME

The minutes of the meeting of the Executive Board held at Teachers College and dated March 27, 1935 reveal that the Society was still searching for a name. Among the names suggested were the National Society for the Study of School and Society, Society for the Study of Education in Its Social Relationships, National Conference for the Study of School and Society, and the John Dewey Society. "It was finally decided to temporarily call the Society the Association for the Study of Education in its Social Aspects," stated the minutes, giving the Society's address as 32 Washington Place, New York City. Possible themes for the Society's first yearbook were proposed, including "Education for Social Reconstruction," to be focused on the American high school and the nation's youth. It was suggested that later yearbooks examine the controlling forces in education and society. The theme for the first yearbook was deferred, pending the canvassing of various members to identify a theme and committee for the first yearbook. George Frasier, President of Colorado State Teachers College, was elected a fellow of the Society.

The meeting of the Executive Board on May 23, 1935, held at Teachers College, again addressed the need to find an appropriate name for the new Society. It was decided to call the Society "The National Council of School and Society." Possible themes for the Society's yearbooks were discussed, such as "Education in a Planned (or Planning) Society," "The Teacher and Society," "The High School and Society," "The Life and Program of the School," and "The Social Forces Controlling the Schools." It was then decided that the first yearbook would be titled *The Teacher and Society*, with William Kilpatrick as chairman. Kilpatrick was authorized to name the yearbook committee. The Board also authorized Kilpatrick to request a large ballroom for the first annual meeting of the Society to be held in conjunction with the NEA's Department of Superintendence meeting scheduled for St. Louis in February of the following year. Kilpatrick was authorized to plan the program.

At the meeting of the Executive Board on October 28, 1935, held at Teachers College, the question of the naming of the Society came up once again. It was agreed that the new name, pending the approval of the members of the Executive Board who were not present, would be "The John Dewey Society" with the subtitle "For the Study of Education in its Social Relations." A committee on constitutional revision was named, composed of Robert Speer of

The

SOCIAL FRONTIER

A Journal of Educational Criticism and Reconstruction

GEORGE S. COUNTS, *Editor*

Associate Editors

MORDECAI GROSSMAN   NORMAN WOELFEL

Board of Contributors

CHARLES A. BEARD	MERLE CURTI	JOSEPH K. HART
BOYD H. BODE	JOHN DEWEY	BROADUS MITCHELL
GEORGE A. COE	HENRY P. FAIRCHILD	LEWIS MUMFORD

VOLUME II	FEBRUARY, 1936	NUMBER 5

Classroom Teachers Advance

CLASSROOM teachers are reaching for power. Here is one of the most significant tendencies of the period. Teachers are becoming increasingly insistent on speaking for themselves,. on placing representatives from their own number in positions of responsibility, on having a voice in the formulation of the policies of their profession. The time seems to be definitely passing when they were content to follow with complete docility the leadership of persons occupying administrative posts. A few recent happenings will show the trend.

In the Texas State Teachers Association, meeting in December, the classroom teachers failed by only three votes in electing their candidate to lead the Association. The actual vote was 1,206 to 1,203. In New York and Idaho proposals were brought before the state conventions providing for a fifty per cent representation of classroom teachers on committees. While these proposals failed of passage, they reveal the changing temper of the teachers. At the New York meeting a resolution was passed without opposition demanding that teachers be granted "that sort of academic freedom which permits the teacher the complete liberty of political conduct and thought to which he is entitled as an American citizen." In Ohio the teachers are working to increase their representation on the executive board of the state association. The teachers of the State of Washington have taken steps to organize a department of classroom teachers. And in Michigan the teachers have been fighting vigorously for a larger voice in the deliberations of the profession.

This growing consciousness of the classroom teacher is naturally feared and opposed by those administrative elements which in the past have dominated the profession. But the far-sighted administrator will not only refuse to oppose this tendency, but will actually encourage it. For a powerful professional organization is absolutely essential at this time for the protection of the educational interests of the

American people. And such an organization cannot come into being as long as the rank and file of teachers are but pawns to be moved about by official authority. In the long run the best interests of school administration will be served through the development of an informed, independent, and courageous body of teachers.

The John Dewey Society

AT THE meeting of the Department of Superintendence in Atlantic City last February a group of educators took steps to launch a society for the study of education in its social aspects and relations. In the meantime the society has been christened The John Dewey Society and three yearbooks have been projected. The first of these studies will deal with the teacher and is being prepared by a strong committee headed by Professor William H. Kilpatrick. It will be completed for the meeting of the Department in 1937.

The new society was named for John Dewey, not because its founders wished to devote themselves to an exposition of the teachings of America's greatest educator and thinker, but rather because they felt that in his life and work he represents the soundest and most hopeful approach to the study of the problems of education. For more than a generation he has proclaimed the social nature of the educative process and emphasized the close interdependence of school and society. Presumably, without being bound by his philosophy, The John Dewey Society will work out of the tradition which John Dewey has done more than any other person to create. Such an organization is badly needed in America today.

The society will make its debut in St. Louis on the afternoon of Sunday, February 23, at the Hotel Jefferson. The subject for discussion at this meeting, which will be open to all persons interested, will be the very timely question of freedom of teaching and the loyalty oaths. The details are given in the announcement on the back page of this issue.

ON THE OCCASION OF ITS
FIRST ANNUAL MEETING

THE JOHN DEWEY SOCIETY
FOR THE STUDY OF EDUCATION
AND CULTURE

Will present a discussion of the topic:

Teachers' Loyalty Oaths — Fascism?

●

SPEAKERS:

Philip F. La Follette
Governor of Wisconsin

William McAndrew

Boyd H. Bode

CHAIRMAN:

William H. Kilpatrick

SUNDAY AFTERNOON, FEBRUARY 23, 1936
2:30 o'clock

AT THE
JEFFERSON HOTEL (The Gold Room)
St. Louis, Missouri

EVERYBODY INVITED

III

ORIGINS AND CONNECTIONS

The membership of the founding group was national in scope.

—Henry Harap

Over the course of its fifty-five year history, only three journal articles have traced the origins of the John Dewey Society. The first of these articles was written by Archibald Anderson in launching the first issue of the journal *Educational Theory* in May, 1951—a journal sponsored jointly by the John Dewey Society and the College of Education of the University of Illinois. Although Anderson's article was devoted mainly to the function of the new journal and educational theory as a field of inquiry, a good portion of the article traced the founding of the Society and its role and activities.

Nineteen years were to pass before a second article appeared in which Henry Harap, who with Jesse Newlon had taken the first steps in organizing the John Dewey Society, pointed out that Archibald Anderson's account had neglected to mention the events of 1934 which led to the birth of the Society (Harap, 1970, p. 157). Anderson also failed to acknowledge the activities of Henry Harap and Jesse Newlon in connection with the formation of the Society.

THE TEACHERS COLLEGE DISCUSSION GROUP
AND THE JOHN DEWEY SOCIETY

In his 1970 article in *Educational Theory*, Henry Harap took issue with Archibald Anderson's account that the "pioneering activity" of the Discussion Group of the faculty in social foundations of education at Teachers College, which met regularly between 1927 and 1934 under the chairmanship of William Kilpatrick "resulted in the establishment of two formal instruments for furthering the social reorientation of education and advancing study of fundamental educational problems. One of these was the magazine, *The Social Frontier.* The other was the John Dewey Society" (Anderson, 1951, p. 10).

From his own file of correspondence and papers, Harap proceeded to chronicle the events of 1934 and early 1935 which led to the organization of the John Dewey Society. Considering that Henry Harap had not even been mentioned in Anderson's article, one could well understand if Harap felt piqued by the omission. But Harap's response was entirely dispassionate. In his opening words, Harap related that he had been in touch with Anderson concerning the omissions regarding the events leading up to the founding of the Society and that Anderson acknowledged that he had been unaware of these events. Harap noted that Anderson wrote to him of his plans to write a more detailed historical account of the Society and that Anderson was planning to ask some of the founding members to prepare personal statements which were to be woven into the narrative. "As far as I know," wrote Harap, "this has not been done, due, I presume, to Mr. Anderson's untimely death" (p. 157). Henry Harap had indeed been patient. Archibald Anderson died in 1965, fourteen years after the publication of his article on the John Dewey Society in *Educational Theory*. Almost six more years were to pass before Harap wrote his account, "The Beginnings of the John Dewey Society," in response to Anderson's article of 1951.

The third article on the origins of the John Dewey Society appeared in *Educational Theory* in 1977 under the authorship of Henry C. Johnson, Jr., who had obtained copies of the correspondence and other materials that Henry Harap had supplied Archibald Anderson in July of 1951—two months after the publication of Anderson's article in *Educational Theory*. (These items are in the John Dewey Society Archives at Southern Illinois University.) In his heavily documented article, Johnson proceeded to chronicle in detail the events in 1934 and 1935 leading to the formation of the Society.

For the most part, Johnson's history corresponded with Harap's article, but Johnson unaccountably made no mention of the issue raised by Harap in holding Anderson in error for tracing the origins of the Society to the pioneering activity of the Kilpatrick Discussion Group at Teachers College. Although Kilpatrick was to play a leading role in the activities of the John Dewey Society, his name was absent from the original lists of persons compiled by Harap and Newlon to be invited to the Cleveland meeting of February 25, 1934. Johnson did not state that the Society was an outgrowth of the Kilpatrick Group, but he claimed that, "With the exception of John Dewey himself, Harrison Elliott, Sidney Hook, Alvin Johnson, E. L. Lindeman, Harry Overstreet, and V. T. Thayer, every member of the *Frontier's* large initial Board of Directors was an original nominee or actual participant in the Dewey Society's founding" (1977, p. 70). This statement by Johnson conflicts with Harap's contention that, "While the beginning of *The Social Frontier*

could be partially traced to the Discussion Group, its influence on the founding of the John Dewey Society was only
peripheral" (1970, p. 159).

According to Harap, who in 1934 had initiated the move
to convene a conference of liberal educators which was to
lead to the formal organization of the John Dewey Society,
only thirteen of the original twenty-eight members of the
Board of Directors of *The Social Frontier* had been invited
to meet with the group of thirty-five to forty educators on
February 25, 1934 to consider the organization of the prospective John Dewey Society (p. 160). Of the sixty-seven
founding members of the Society, eighteen were affiliated
with Teachers College. Considering the preeminent role
of Teachers College in American education at that time,
such a strong representation should not be surprising.
Nevertheless, the founding members were from eighteen
colleges and universities, eight school systems, one educational association, and three educational publications.
Harap noted that "The membership of the Board of Directors of *The Social Frontier* was limited to New York City and
vicinity and its purpose was the publication of a journal
of educational criticism and reconstruction," whereas "the
membership of the founding group of the John Dewey
Society was national in scope and its purpose was to organize a society 'to discharge our responsibility in the present
era of social change'" (pp. 158, 159–160).

The original Board of Directors of *The Social Frontier*
soon became aware of the need to extend its representation geographically and ideologically, so that within a year
after the appearance of the first issue of the journal, it was
announced that eighteen members had been added to the
Board (*The Social Frontier*, 1, May, 1935, p. 8). Thirteen of the
new members were from outside New York City, including

Henry Harap. This lends support to Harap's comments on the differences in the makeup of the founding group of *The Social Frontier*, which grew out of the Teachers College Discussion Group and that of the John Dewey Society, which had national representation from its inception.

Nevertheless, several founding members of the John Dewey Society were to contribute articles to *The Social Frontier* throughout the years of its existence (1934–1939). Moreover, as discussed later, the Society was to become the sponsor of *The Social Frontier* during 1937–1938.

Anderson's error in seeing the John Dewey Society as an outgrowth of the Teachers College Discussion Group under Kilpatrick can be traced to the source of his information, namely the account on the origins of the John Dewey Society in Harold Rugg's textbook, *Foundations for American Education* (1947). In Rugg's words:

> The new study of society launched by Veblen, Turner, et al., was bearing fruit—in education as well as in government. In the 1930s the new educational organ on the social front was *The Social Frontier* and the new organization was the John Dewey Society for the Study of Education and Culture. Both of these new instruments were fashioned by a little nucleus of professors of the social foundations of education at Teachers College. . . . As early as 1927 we formed our little Discussion Group around Dr. Kilpatrick as chairman. (p. 578)

In *The Transformation of the School* (1961), Lawrence Cremin also draws from Rugg's *Foundations for American Education* in stating that "The Kilpatrick Group also provided the nucleus of the John Dewey Society for the Study of Education and Culture, organized in 1935" (p. 229).

Rugg's perceptions undoubtedly were honestly recorded. However, the facts as presented in the documentation provided by Henry Harap clearly reveal that Rugg was in error. Unfortunately, Rugg's statement portraying the John Dewey Society as an instrument fashioned by the Kilpatrick Discussion Group at Teachers College has been perpetuated over the years by a number of established scholars. For example, in *An Educational History of the American People* (1967), Adolphe E. Meyer wrote:

> Out of the era's social and economic shambles came the John Dewey Society for the Study of Education and Culture. Come into being in 1935, it had its start in a small circle of savants from Columbia's Teachers College. In its new incarnation, however, it stretched over the whole republic, with members scattered from ocean to ocean and from border to border, several of whom, moreover, were touted very highly for the light they had flashed on social and economic problems. (pp. 319–320)

Other scholars have continued to link the origins of the Society to a group of educators mainly from the New York City area who met in New York in 1935, whereas over sixty percent of those who participated in that meeting were from outside the New York City area. In his admirable biography of Dewey (1973), George Dykhuizen erroneously states that the members of the group that established the Society at the 1935 meeting were mostly from the New York City area:

> A notable honor came to Dewey in 1935 when a group of professional educators mostly from the New York City area founded an organization dedicated to the study of education and culture named The John Dewey Society. After a modest start, the society expanded its membership till eventually it included persons from throughout the nation as well as some foreign countries. (p. 280)

From the time that Henry Harap and Jesse Newlon compiled their first lists of educators to be invited to participate in the meetings of 1934 up to the meeting of February 24, 1935, when the John Dewey Society was formally launched, efforts were made to secure national representation of educational leaders. Indeed the letter of invitation to the historic meeting of 1935 (Harap, p. 160), specified that railroad and Pullman fares would be pooled by all (with the obvious intent of not placing an undue burden of travel expenses for those coming from outside the region of the meeting).

It will be recalled that Henry Harap was impelled to write his account of the beginnings of the John Dewey Society in view of the failure of existing accounts to trace the organization's origins to the seminal meetings of 1934 (and to the key roles played by Harap and Newlon in convening these meetings), along with the error in the existing accounts in portraying the John Dewey Society as an instrument fashioned by the Kilpatrick Discussion Group at Teachers College. As pointed out, despite Harap's published account, noted scholars have continued to draw from Harold Rugg's *Foundations for American Education* in perpetuating these errors and in failing to mention the critical meetings of 1934 that led to the formation of the John Dewey Society.

Gunnar Myrdal has pointed out that eventually the "facts kick," thereby creating the power of correction in social scholarship (1969, p. 40). In this vein, appropriate recognition must be given to Henry Harap and Jesse Newlon, and to the national contingent of sixty-seven educational leaders who became the founding members of the John Dewey Society.

IV

THE LAST OF THE FOUNDERS

If progressive education is to be genuinely progressive, it must face squarely and courageously every issue.

—George S. Counts

In an exchange of correspondence between Henry Harap and Archibald Anderson, following Anderson's article in the inaugural issue of *Educational Theory* (May, 1951), Anderson had written that he planned to ask some of the original members of the John Dewey Society to prepare statements which would be woven into a detailed historical account of the beginnings of the Society. Unfortunately, Anderson did not carry out his plans.

Thirty-four years were to pass before the idea of contacting the surviving founders was raised. The occasion was the meeting of the Executive Board on February 27, 1985 at the Fairmont Hotel in Denver. Although the date marked the fiftieth anniversary of the Society, no special publication or event had been arranged to commemorate the occasion. The discussion that ensued centered on identifying the surviving founding members with the prospect of contacting them and eliciting their personal reminiscences and perspectives related to the beginnings of the Society and significant events during its early years, along with any pertinent accounts of their own professional activities

during that period. One suggestion was that formal inter-
views be conducted for the purpose of compiling a kind of
oral history to be published for the Society's membership.
In reviewing the list of sixty-seven founding members, it
was determined that the following were alive and active:
Hollis L. Caswell, Donald P. Cottrell, Edgar Dale, Paul R.
Hanna, Sidney Hook, Theodore M. Newcomb, and Ralph
W. Tyler. Of these seven, I was personally acquainted with
Caswell, Dale, Hanna, and Tyler.

In the efforts to contact the seven individuals, it was
learned that Theodore Newcomb had died on December
28, 1984 and that Edgar Dale had died later that same winter. During the summer of 1985, the author visited with
Paul Hanna and Ralph Tyler to discuss the project. Both
indicated that it would be more feasible, in consideration
of time, distance, and expense, for the surviving founding
members to respond in the form of a letter.

In the fall of 1985 letters were sent to Hollis Caswell,
Donald Cottrell, Paul Hanna, Sidney Hook, and Ralph
Tyler. Enclosed with the letter were copies of two articles
published on the origins of the John Dewey Society ("The
Beginnings of the John Dewey Society" by Henry Harap
in *Educational Theory,* Spring 1970, and "Reflective Thought
and Practical Application: The Origins of the John Dewey
Society" by Henry C. Johnson, Jr. in *Educational Theory,*
Winter 1977). The letter made the following request:

> . . . I am asking that you read the enclosed materials and
> respond with an extended statement of personal remi-
> niscences, perspectives, anecdotes and/or discussion of
> events relating to the beginnings of the Society and its
> early years of operation—including an account of your
> own professional activities at that time. . . .
>
> I am deliberately leaving the approach open and
> informal because I feel that the publication will be most

widely appealing to the members of the Society and to our profession at large if the writing reflects your own style and character.

Hollis Caswell and Donald Cottrell responded promptly. Caswell stated that he really had little to do with the actual founding of the Society. However, in a follow-up telephone conversation with him it was learned that he was fighting off a severe and painful illness and was in no condition to give the project any attention. Hollis Caswell died on November 22, 1988 at the age of eighty-seven.

Although Paul Hanna had agreed to respond to the letter, he too suffered a series of severe health setbacks at the time. Fortunately, he made a good recovery, but he never did get around to sending the author his reminiscences of the early days of the John Dewey Society. Paul Hanna died on April 8, 1988 at the age of eighty-five.

Ralph Tyler responded with a letter dated November 4, 1985 suggesting that we arrange a meeting to discuss the project further. In that letter, Tyler alluded to the differences between the article by Henry Harap and the one by Henry Johnson, Jr. on the founding of the John Dewey Society. In that letter Tyler states, "What I remember seems quite different in its interpretation from that of Johnson but in fact verifies and parallels Harap's comments."

On November 20, 1985 Ralph Tyler and the author met for dinner in New York City to discuss this modest project. Tyler commented that he could not add much in the way of details to the historic accounts published by Henry Harap (1970) and Henry C. Johnson (1977), but he reiterated that he was fully in agreement with Harap's article and differed with Johnson's account alluding to the prominent role played by the Board of Directors of *The Social Frontier* in the founding of the Society. (See Tyler's letter of November 4,

1985.) As discussed earlier, in his account of the early history of the John Dewey Society, Henry Harap stressed that the influence of the Teachers College Discussion Group and the Board of *The Social Frontier* in connection with the founding of the John Dewey Society "was only peripheral" (1970, p. 159).

Tyler offered that he would like to focus his written comments on the activities of the founding members who met informally but regularly as a discussion group on or near the campus of Ohio State University, and that he might offer some observations concerning the social crisis of the times. Five of the founding members were at Ohio State in 1935. Henry Harap was to join the Ohio State faculty for the 1936–1937 academic years, and Donald Cottrell was to come to Ohio State in 1946.

Tyler sent the author his account, "The John Dewey Society's Early Activities as I Recall Them," with a cover letter dated February 3, 1986.

Realizing that no response was received from Sidney Hook, it was learned by telephone that he had not received the letter along with the enclosed articles by Harap and Johnson. This material was sent to him immediately, and he responded promptly with his letter dated February 20, 1986, just before he was to undergo eye surgery. Although it was determined later that Sidney Hook was not a founding member, his recollections as an early and active member of the Society point revealingly to the indoctrination controversy, as propounded by the reconstructionists, which became of great concern to many members of the Society as well as to Dewey himself. Hook's recollections on this issue are corroborated in Ralph Tyler's more detailed statement on some of the concerns of the founding members of the Society during a time of unprecedented social crisis.

All told, letters were obtained from Donald P. Cottrell, Sidney Hook, and Ralph W. Tyler.

V

RECOLLECTIONS AND RETROSPECTIONS

> Both Dewey and I were troubled by some passages in
> Counts' "Dare the Schools . . . ," both on social and his-
> torical grounds, and because they lent themselves to a
> kind of indoctrination which we—and Counts himself
> at heart—really opposed.
>
> —Sidney Hook

In his account of the times in which the nation was in the
depths of the Great Depression, Sidney Hook recalls in
his letter that, "Of course, the general feeling was that the
economic system was completely *finished* but there was
no unanimity or even general agreement on what was to
replace it." He goes on to state, "As I recall, *my* function
was to act as a critic of the somewhat unguarded statements of the new society which sounded incompatible
with the assumptions of educational and political democracy." In his cover letter of February 3, 1986, Ralph Tyler
makes this similarly revealing statement: ". . . at that time,
the Ohio State Members (of the John Dewey Society) felt
that many of the members in New York were proposing
actions contrary to our notion of the role of education in a
democratic society."

RECONSTRUCTIONISTS AND EXPERIMENTALISTS

The concerns expressed in the letters from both Sidney Hook and Ralph Tyler reflect the differences between the radical views of the reconstructionists, as advanced by George S. Counts, and the more moderate views of the experimentalists who constituted the majority membership of the Society and with whom Hook and Tyler identified themselves. Nevertheless, in recalling the indoctrination issue, Hook makes this revealing statement in his letter: "Both Dewey and I were troubled by some passages in Counts' 'Dare the Schools Rebuild Society?' both on social and historical grounds, and because they lent themselves to a kind of indoctrination which we—and Counts himself at heart—really opposed." (The actual title of Counts' pamphlet was *Dare the School Build a New Social Order?*) One of the passages to which Hook obviously refers is the following:

> If Progressive Education is to be genuinely progressive, it must emancipate itself from the influence of this class (upper-middle, liberal), face squarely and courageously every social issue, come to grips with life in all its stark reality, establish an organic relation with the community, develop a realistic and comprehensive theory of welfare, fashion a compelling vision of human destiny, and become less frightened than it is today at the bogies of *imposition* and *indoctrination*. (1932, pp. 9–10)

In his account of the times, submitted to me with his letter of February 3, 1986, Ralph Tyler recalls how the members of the Ohio State group were stimulated by Counts' challenge, but were concerned about the indoctrination question. In this connection, Tyler recalls that Boyd Bode often joined the group in the discussions and that Bode viewed the proposal for educational reconstruction by Counts as indoctrination rather than democratic education.

Indeed, both Dewey and Bode repeatedly took issue with Counts and the reconstructionists on the indoctrination question. An article by Dewey in *The Social Frontier* of October, 1934, and one by Bode in the January, 1935 issue of that same magazine, clearly pointed to the critical difference and inherent conflict between prescribing or imposing beliefs on the learner, and reflectively considering issues and possible solutions with the learner. In an address before the NEA in 1934, titled "Education for a Changing Social Order," Dewey stressed that it would be revolution enough if educators were to recognize the reality of social change and to act upon that recognition in the schools.

Interestingly, as mentioned earlier, Boyd Bode was not a founding member of the John Dewey Society, despite the fact that six of the founding members were on the Ohio State faculty—O. G. Brim, Edgar Dale, H. Gordon Hullfish, Rudolph Lindquist, I. Keith Tyler, and Ralph W. Tyler. In his account of the beginnings of the Society, Henry Harap included a list of sixty founding members taken from a letter dated February 6, 1935 and signed by George S. Counts, Jesse H. Newlon, and Harold Rugg. The letter states, "There is a remote possibility that some names have been omitted from this list." Harap was able to find two omissions (R. B. Raup and Ralph Spence). As noted earlier, five other names had been omitted, making a total of sixty-seven persons who were originally identified as charter fellows of the Society. Harap also listed Gordon Hullfish as being affiliated with the Dalton School, although biographical references reveal that Hullfish was on the faculty of Ohio State while he also was serving as director of curriculum construction (high school) at Dalton.

Regarding the conspicuous absence of Boyd Bode among the founding members of the John Dewey Society, there can be no grounds for speculation that his absence stemmed from ideological differences since Bode was a featured speaker at the first annual meeting of the Society held in St. Louis. Moreover, the founding group of progressive educators was highly diverse, and as Harap pointed out, "No single economic or educational theory was accepted as the official position of the whole group" (1970, p. 159).

HARD TIMES—FROM ECONOMIC DEPRESSION
TO IDEOLOGICAL REPRESSION

The letters of response from Donald P. Cottrell, Sidney Hook, and Ralph W. Tyler are presented in chapter 6 along with brief biographies of these respondents.

The letters from Sidney Hook and Ralph Tyler reflect on the hard times of the Great Depression when the John Dewey Society was founded, and the pervasive concern of progressive educators for the survival of democracy in the midst of economic and social collapse. As noted earlier, both Hook and Tyler single out the indoctrination controversy in connection with the challenge issued by George S. Counts.

The letter of Donald Cottrell recounts the difficult years in keeping the Dewey Society solvent during which time the Society ceased publication of its influential yearbooks. Cottrell offers some fascinating perspectives on the storm of McCarthyism created by Harold Rugg's Bode Lecture at Ohio State in the summer of 1951, and the decision to hold the meeting of the Society's Executive Board, under Kilpatrick's leadership, in Columbus (instead of New York) where threats to academic freedom had reached crisis proportions. Cottrell relates how Kilpatrick acted on Cottrell's suggestion and persuaded Benjamin Fine, education editor of *The New York Times,* to investigate the situation at Ohio State University, with the result that the ensuing publicity called international attention to the issue of academic freedom. The powerful behind-the-scenes role of the John Dewey Society in combating McCarthyism is one of the unsung stories of that shameful era, and Cottrell is all too modest in recounting his own role.

In the spring of 1951, *The New York Times* ran a series of articles on the threats to freedom of thought and speech gripping the nation's colleges in the wake of the Cold War and McCarthyism. It was reported that students and faculty were becoming increasingly reluctant to take a humanitarian viewpoint on issues for fear of being associated with communism (May 10, 1951, pp. 1, 28).

In July 1951, Harold Rugg, professor emeritus at Teachers College and a founding member of the John Dewey Society, delivered the Boyd Bode Lecture at Ohio State. Rugg's message for school and society was not radically leftist in any sense, but he and his school textbooks had come under attack of right-wing organizations and the conservative press during the early 1940s for allegedly subversive views. Although he and his textbooks were repeatedly cleared of the charges, the textbooks were banned in schools across the nation *(Publishers Weekly,* June 22, 1940, p. 2345). Following Rugg's lecture at Ohio State, the university's Board of Trustees condemned the College of Education for having invited Rugg to the campus. The Board held that Rugg was unfit to speak on campus since he was espousing un-American propaganda. "The function of the university is teaching, not indoctrinations," declared the

Board (*New York Times,* September 5, 1951, p. 29). The Board then empowered the president of the university to screen all outside speakers before invitations were to be extended. Donald P. Cottrell, then Dean of the College of Education, openly attacked the Board ruling. "Our faculty members consider the screening regulations an unwarranted interference with our obligations and responsibilities as professional men and women," Cottrell was quoted as saying in a *New York Times* article (October 25, 1951, p. 44). A feature story on academic freedom that November quoted William Kilpatrick as condemning the ruling at Ohio State for embracing "totalitarian methods" (*The New York Times,* November 17, 1951, p. 44). Within four months following its ruling, the Board retreated in apparent embarrassment by the ensuing publicity and placed the responsibility for speaker screening with the faculty, although the president was to be "consulted" in cases of "doubt" (*The New York Times,* December 23, 1951, Sec. 4, p. 9). Despite the retreat by the Board, the stipulation that the university president was to be "consulted" in cases of "doubt" remained a point of contention with the faculty. Moreover, the bitter residue of the Rugg episode was to remain with the university for years to come.

Cottrell's letter brings to light an unrecorded and highly significant event in the history of the John Dewey Society. Whereas the press had been used previously by right-wing elements to attack academic freedom, the Executive Board of the John Dewey Society had acted to enlist the press in exposing the growing threat to such freedom.

None of the writers of the letters seeks to glorify the early years of the John Dewey Society. But it is clear that they and other founding members of the Society were vitally concerned with and engaged in the great educational and social issues.

VI

THE LETTERS

If the school believes that its primary function is to teach people to adjust to society it will strongly emphasize obedience to the present authorities, loyalty to the present forms and traditions, skills in carrying on the present techniques of life; whereas if it emphasizes the revolutionary function of the school it will be more concerned with critical analysis, ability to meet new problems, independence and self-direction, freedom, and self-discipline.

—Ralph W. Tyler, Basic *Principles of Curriculum and Instruction*, 1949

Ralph W. Tyler was born in Chicago in 1902. He earned his A.B. degree at Doane College in Nebraska (1921), his A.M. at the University of Nebraska (1923), and his Ph.D. at the University of Chicago (1927). He was a high school teacher in South Dakota. From 1922 to 1927 he was an assistant supervisor of science teaching at the University of Nebraska. Upon earning his doctorate, he joined the faculty at the University of North Carolina. From 1929 to 1938 he was on the faculty of the College of Education at Ohio State University where he also served as a research associate in the Bureau of Educational Research. From 1938 to 1948 he chaired the Department of Education and served as university examiner at the University of Chicago. Tyler served as Director of evaluation in the Eight-Year Study from 1934 to 1942, and Director of the cooperative study in general education for the American Council on Education from 1930 to 1946. He became Dean of the Division of Social Sciences at the University of Chicago in 1948. In 1953 he became the founding Director of the Center for Advanced Study in the Behavioral Sciences. Upon becoming Director Emeritus of the Center for Advanced Study, he served as President of the System Development Foundation. He was a member of the National Science Board and was first President of the National Academy of Education. In 1988 Tyler took the appointment of Distinguished Scholar in residence in the School of Education at Stanford University.

2233 Shiloh Avenue
Milpitas, CA 95035
November 4, 1985

Dear Dan:

   I have delayed a very long time in replying to your letter inviting me to write my recollections about the early days of the John Dewey Society.

   The delay is due to my effort to recall and to assess the possible significance of what I can recall. Since what I remember seems quite different in its interpretation from that of Johnson but in fact verifies and parallels Harap's comments, I am uncertain about what my report could contribute. I should like to talk with you about this before deciding on writing such a report.

   I hope you will not think I am too lazy to write. But I don't wish to write something which could have little meaning to the Society's members.

   Is there a possible time and place we could get together to talk about this?

   With warm regards,

              Sincerely,
              Ralph

SYSTEM DEVELOPMENT FOUNDATION
181 LYTTON AVENUE, SUITE 210, PALO ALTO, CALIFORNIA 94301–1096
(415) 328–5120

February 3, 1986

Dr. Daniel Tanner
Highwood Road
Somerset, N.J. 08873

Dear Dr. Tanner:

You asked me to write down what I could recall of the early days of the John Dewey Society. The enclosed paper is the result. It doesn't seem startling or even very interesting but at that time, the Ohio State members felt that many of the members in New York were proposing actions contrary to our notion of the role of education in a democratic society.

If you see any points where elaboration might make this more interesting, please let me know.

With Warm Regards,

Sincerely,

Ralph W. Tyler
President

The John Dewey Society's Early Activities as I Recall Them

By Ralph W. Tyler

As Henry Harap reported[1] the society was founded during the midst of the Great Depression. Throughout the nation, leaders in business, agriculture and politics were recommending actions designed to end the economic and social disaster and to rebuild the economy and reconstruct the social order.

The American Youth Commission had been established by the American Council in Education to report on the plight of American youth and to recommend actions to improve their condition.

Its report, *How Fare American Youth?*, had enhanced support of the bills in Congress to establish the National Youth Administration and to provide funds for the work-study programs for young people who wished to continue their education. Legislation was also enacted to establish the Civilian Conservation Corps for those unemployed young who did not wish to continue their education in school. The CCC provided work for them in maintaining and improving the national parks.

Neither the NYA nor the CCC were under the local or state school systems. The NYA established state directors who were directly responsible to the federal directors and the CCC was administered by the Army and guided by an official from the U.S. Office of Education. It is understandable that educators in schools and colleges felt that they had been overlooked and had a contribution to make in reforming education and reconstructing the social order to eliminate such depressions in the future.

This concern of educators and the founding of the John Dewey Society are well described by Harap. I want to report on the activities of the charter members who were at the Ohio State University or nearby. These were Fred Bair, Superintendent of Schools, Shaker Heights, Ohio; Lawrence Sears of Ohio Wesleyan University; and Orville Brim, Edgar Dale, Gordon Hullfish, Rudolph Lindquist, and Ralph Tyler, all of Ohio State University.

After the Society had been established this group in and near Columbus often met informally for lunch or dinner at the Faculty Club or the Dutch Mill Restaurant which was just across High Street from the Education Building. Less often we met on Saturdays or late afternoon. In our early sessions, we discussed the possible activities of the Society and assessed the probable consequences of each.

We were stimulated by George Counts' challenge, "Dare the School Build a New Social Order," but we were very critical of the idea. In an address John Dewey delivered in 1936 to the Michigan School Masters Club, he said, "It is possible to exaggerate greatly the direct influence of schools upon formation of social and institutional life. It is not possible to exaggerate their responsibility with reference to the effect of what they do upon the formation of the attitudes, intellectual or moral, of the youth who are to determine the direction future society will take."

Boyd Bode often joined in our discussions. He characterized Counts' proposal as indoctrination rather than democratic education. Our discussions generally led to the view that the proper role of the school was to help students to understand the great potential of a democratic society and to analyze the problems faced in attaining that potential. The school's role, we argued is to help students learn how to solve the problems they encounter. It is not to give to them our pet solutions. The problems of tomorrow cannot be anticipated in detail and with clarity now, and our attempts to define them and to provide solutions inhibit the development in students of the ability to identify, attack and solve the problems that arise in the future. We were not unanimous in our treatment of this issue. Hence, it was a subject we frequently debated.

Another one was the role of subject matter in a curriculum focused on problem solving rather than on memorizing information. We had observed those "progressives" who focused their curriculum solely on the presumed or ascertained interests of their students to the neglect of the conditions and events in the environment with which they must cope. However, this one-sided concern had been corrected by many progressive schools as they recognized the social functions of schooling. But still many progressive educators had no place in their curriculum planning for subject-matter content. Yet we know that John Dewey had defined subject matter as the ideas, information, skills, and attitudes that are relevant to solving the problem on which the students are working. We believed that the reconstruction of society by generations to come would require much subject matter to guide their thinking and action.

It seems to me, as I look back upon the early days of the John Dewey Society, that the members in the Ohio State University were reexamining and reinterpreting Dewey. The founding of the society had stimulated our interest in seeking guidance from him and his writings.

We believed that the desired reconstruction of society would be more likely to develop from schools and colleges incorporating Dewey's main ideas in their educational efforts, than from a revolution focusing primarily on the restructuring and reorganization of society.

SIDNEY HOOK (1902–1989)

Not all critics read Dewey with the aim of understanding him, and, judging by the volume, quality, and substance of most popular criticisms of Dewey, much of it seems written by people who have not read him.
—Sidney Hook, *Education & The Taming of Power*, 1973

Sidney Hook was born in New York City and did his undergraduate work at CCNY (B.S., 1923). He pursued his graduate studies at Columbia University (M.A., 1926; Ph.D., 1927). From 1923 to 1928 he was a teacher in the New York City public schools. Over a period spanning forty-two years, he served on the philosophy faculty of New York University. For twenty-one of those years Sidney Hook chaired the all-university department of philosophy at NYU. From 1969 until his death on July 12, 1989 at age eighty-seven, he was a senior research fellow at the Hoover Institution on War, Revolution, and Peace at Stanford University. Hook was the author of a score of books on philosophy and education including *Political Power and*

Personal Freedom (1959), *Education for Modern Man* (1963), *Academic Freedom and Academic Anarchy* (1970), *Philosophy and Public Policy* (1980), and *Marxism and Beyond* (1983). He was the recipient of the Presidential Medal of Freedom (1985), several honorary doctorates from Maine to California, and was a fellow of the American Academy of Arts and Sciences and the American Academy of Education. Right-wing conservatives and fundamentalists attacked him for his secular humanism, while those from the Left attacked him as neoconservative. A student of John Dewey at Columbia University, "Hook never tired of saying that there were no absolutes. He believed that all ideas had to be tested against the reality of experience" (*The New York Times*, July 14, 1989, p. D15).

HOOVER INSTITUTION
ON WAR, REVOLUTION AND PEACE

Stanford, California 94305–2323

February 20, 1986

Prof. Daniel Tanner
Graduate School of Education
Rutgers University
10 Seminary Place
New Brunswick, New Jersey 08903

Dear Professor Tanner:

Thank you for your letter of February 13th together with a copy of your letter of November 14, 1985 which unfortunately I never received. That is why your telephone call was such a surprise since I did not know what you were referring to.

I am grateful to you for thinking of me in connection with the project and I shall do my best to dredge up any memories about a distant event years ago. Unfortunately I am scheduled to undergo another cataract operation in a few days and shall be unable to get to read all the material and write about it—in the event I recall anything relevant—for some time.

My memories of the details of the origin of the John Dewey Society are very vague. I was intellectually and educationally quite close to George Counts, Jack Childs, William Kilpatrick and Jesse Newlon because of my relationship to Dewey, but I was closer to *The Social Frontier* than to the formal structure of the John Dewey Society.

Of course, the general feeling was that the economic system was completely finished but there was no unanimity or even general agreement on what was to replace it. The term "collectivism" was not defined, nor the degree of "planning". Counts and others had been very much influenced by the Soviet Union but were already becoming aware of the totalitarian aspects of Soviet Communism. As I recall, *my* function was to act as a critic of the somewhat unguarded statements about the new society which sounded incompatible with the assumptions of educational and political democracy. This I did mostly in conversations with George Counts and Jack Childs.

Prof. Tanner
February 20, 1986
Page 2

Both Dewey and I were troubled by some passages in Counts "Dare the Schools Rebuild Society?" both on social and historical grounds, and because they lent themselves to a kind of indoctrination which we—and Counts himself at heart—really opposed. Without immodesty I believe my long criticisms of the Soviet Union after its doctrine of Social Fascism helped bring Hitler to power, accelerated George Counts' penetration of the rhetorical facade that disguised the outrageous totalitarian practices of the U.S.S.R.

But I shall be writing more perhaps later.

Sincerely yours,

Sidney Hook
Emeritus Professor of Philosophy
New York University
Senior Research Fellow
Hoover Institution

I served as Secretary-Treasurer of the John Dewey Society for a good many years—just how many, I don't know. I presume that I was elected to that post by the Executive Board around 1937 when the publication of the Yearbook series was begun, for I remember dealing with Ordway Tead of Harpers Publishers on a good number of those books. I left Teachers College to come to The Ohio State University as Dean of the large College of Education in September, 1946, and soon after my arrival I remember being told by my faculty colleague, "Hank" Hullfish, that we would have to get busy to bail out the John Dewey Society which had ceased its publication of Yearbooks and had run a sizable deficit. After a painful push for personal contributions from a few leaders of the Society, we accomplished that mission. The intervention of World War II interrupted Society operations for me, and therefore I do not know what happened on that front, as my duties at Teachers College expanded to about three times their former amount.

I do remember that I was still Secretary-Treasurer after coming to Ohio State. For one early year here we held a John Dewey Society Executive Board meeting in my office here in Columbus. It seems that with a shortage of funds we persuaded Dr. Kilpatrick, our Chairman, to come here, rather than for all of the other Board members to go to New York. We could save a good deal of travel money that way.

One reason for that meeting being memorable for me was that it occurred soon after a big "McCarthyite" fuss had broken out here over a Summer Quarter lecture (on the Boyd H. Bode Fund) by Harold Rugg. Before beginning our John Dewey Society business that morning, Dr. Kilpatrick asked me to brief the group as to what was going on, which I did. Dr. Kilpatrick shook his head in dismay and asked if there might be anything he could do. I said that there most certainly would be, namely, that on his return to New York he could call "Benny" Fine, the Education Editor of the New York Times, and tell him whatever he was pleased to say. He did so and in another day Dr. Fine was here. The ensuing publicity resulted in a worldwide academic freedom discussion and in our O.S.U. Board of Trustees passing a "Speaker Screening Rule" with the University President having responsibility to pre-censor off-campus speakers. It took years to contain that thrust here in an acceptable way.

I know that the Society has continued constructive work through the years, although I have not been able to be a part of it. I have been pre-occupied with a host of other activities—the presidency or chairmanship of sundry groups, including the American Association of Colleges for Teacher Education, the Land Grant Colleges Association Commission on Teacher Education, the N.E.A. National Commission on Teacher Education and Professional Standards, etc. I am aware of the John Dewey Society Center for publications at Carbondale, Illinois, the meetings and lectures in connection with the annual conferences of the A.A.C.T.E. which happily continue today. I hope that there may be continuing cooperation with the National Society of Professors of Education.

I doubt that these rambling notes can have any value to you for publication, for which I am sorry. Personal and family difficulties have diverted most of my professional efforts in the thirteen years since my retirement. Please forgive me and accept my best wishes for what you are doing.

Sincerely yours,

Donald P. Cottrell

NOTES

1. Harap, "The Beginnings of the John Dewey *Society*," *Educational Theory*, Vol. 20, Spring 1970.

VII

THIS ORDEAL OF DEMOCRACY

> Hanna was associated with Hollis L. Caswell . . . who was associated with the John Dewey Society. . . . The John Dewey Society was associated with the names of such radical educators as Professors Counts, Kilpatrick and Speer who were associated with organizations suspected of being communist fronts.
>
> —Report to the California Senate Investigating Committee on Education

The action by the Executive Board of the John Dewey Society concerning the infamous attack on academic freedom following Harold Rugg's Bode Lecture at Ohio State University in the summer of 1951 was an important, but relatively unknown episode in the Society's long tradition of upholding freedom of inquiry. It will be recalled that the first formal meeting of the John Dewey Society, held in 1936, was devoted to teachers' loyalty oaths and academic freedom. The defense of academic freedom was to be one of the focal concerns addressed in the Society's yearbooks issued from 1937 to 1963.

TEXTBOOK CENSORSHIP

Among the founding members of the John Dewey Society, Harold Rugg and Paul Hanna were to stand out for creating

49

textbooks and supplementary curricular materials that were widely used in the schools. The assault against Rugg and his social studies and history textbooks began during the late 1930s when right-wing organizations labeled the texts as un-American. Articles in popular magazines such as *Time, Saturday Evening Post, Forbes,* and *Nation's Business* were including the Rugg textbooks in their attacks against progressive education. By the early 1940s, Rugg's textbooks were undergoing full eclipse as school boards and adminis- trators were ordering their removal and destruction. In his obituary in *The New York Times* following Rugg's death on May 17, 1960 at the age of seventy-four, it was noted that a *Times* reviewer of Rugg's books had found it "extraordi- nary" that his books should be so fiercely denounced. The obituary cited the reviewer as writing that Rugg "believes that the attacks are significant and ominous features of the present age, this 'ordeal of democracy'" (May 18, 1960, p. 41). The obituary also contained this quotation of Rugg:

> A democracy can exist on no other basis than the fullest, frankest study of its problems by all of the people. Hence, a full account of American life, unbiased as is humanly possible to make it, should be studied. No problems and issues should be covered up or kept away from young people.

As mentioned earlier, Paul Hanna also figured notably as a target for attack, namely in connection with the *Building America* series of supplementary social studies texts during the 1940s—sponsored by the Society for Curriculum Study (Newman, 1960). The Society for Curriculum Study had grown out of the efforts of Henry Harap beginning in 1928 to create a medium of exchange of ideas on curriculum making. In 1932, the group became known as the Society for Curriculum Study. (The Society was to merge with the NEA's Department of Supervision and Directors of Instruction to become the Association for Supervision and Curriculum Development in 1941.) With Henry Harap serving as chairman of the Executive Committee of the Society for Curriculum Study, much of the 1933 Annual Meeting was devoted to the curriculum and the social crisis.

At the 1934 Annual Meeting of the Society for Curriculum Study, the following year, held in Cleveland, Henry Harap proposed that the Society should pool its resources and create materials to help students in the study of social problems. Herbert Bruner of Teachers College submitted a proposal for the project, and Paul Hanna outlined his proposed plans for *Building America*. Within months, the first Editorial Board for the project was assembled with Paul Hanna as chairman.

Five of the six members of the first Editorial Board of *Building America* were to become founders of the John Dewey Society (Paul R. Hanna, Hollis L. Caswell, C. L. Cushman, Edgar Dale, and Harold Hand). Jesse Newlon joined the Editorial Board later that year. With modest voluntary contributions from the members of the Society for Curriculum Study, the first issue, *Housing* (1935), was launched. This led to grants from the General Education Board during the early years of the *Building America* series. In 1940 it was being published by the Americana Corporation, and by 1945 the sales of the monthly paperback were over a million copies per issue. Annual editions were published in hardback. Over the years from 1935 to 1948, the widely acclaimed series included ninety-one issues on such problem-focused topics as: *Food, Health, Power, Youth Faces the World, Our Constitution, Social Security, We Consumers, Education, War or Peace, Crime, Civil Liberties, Women,*

Advertising, Italian Americans, Our Water Resources, and *Our Land Resources.*

By 1945 the *Building America* series was under full attack by the conservative press and ultra-right-wing groups and politicians who sought to portray the texts as un-American. With Paul Hanna at Stanford, the locus of attack was mainly in California where the texts were targeted for scrutiny by the State Joint Legislative Fact-Finding Committee on Un-American Activities. As in the case of Harold Rugg's textbooks, right-wing groups sought to eliminate the social studies from the school curriculum and the examination of social issues in favor of a return to the fundamentals and the study of American history through factual subject matter and patriotic treatment.

Appointed by the California Senate Investigating Committee on Education to evaluate the *Building America* series was Richard E. Combs, who had served as counsel for various committees of the legislature in investigating subversive activities. When Combs could not substantiate the allegations that Hanna and the other members of the Editorial Board of *Building America* were affiliated with "communist-front" organizations, he proceeded to make the case that they had been "fooled" by others who had such affiliations. He pointed out that Hanna was associated with Hollis L. Caswell, also on the Editorial Board of *Building America,* who was associated with the John Dewey Society for the Study of Education and Culture. (Combs had failed to recognize that Hanna had been a founding member of the Dewey Society.) In turn, stated Combs, the John Dewey Society was associated with the names of such "radical educators" as "Professors Counts, Kilpatrick and Speer" who were associated with organizations that were suspected of being "communist fronts." (Robert Speer of

New York City also was a founding member of the Dewey Society.)

Despite the failure to prove any of the allegations against the Board and against the material in the *Building America* series, and despite the continued endorsement of the series by the California Curriculum Commission and approval by the California Board of Education, the notoriety caused sales to plummet as the series was being removed from the schools. Americana withdrew as publisher. The last issue of *Building America* appeared at the end of 1948.

VIII

THE JOHN DEWEY SOCIETY
AND *THE SOCIAL FRONTIER*

... ideological problems of an ideological age
—Lawrence A. Cremin

In 1932 the National Society of College Teachers of Education appointed a committee to prepare a yearbook on the philosophy of education. The committee members were William Kilpatrick (chairman), John Dewey, John L. Childs, and R. B. Raup of Teachers College, Boyd H. Bode and H. Gordon Hullfish of Ohio State University, and V. T. Thayer of the Ethical Culture Schools. All but Dewey and Bode were to be among the founding members of the John Dewey Society. Although the charge to the committee was to prepare a yearbook on the philosophy of education, the committee decided to address the yearbook to the emergency conditions of the Great Depression and its impact on the educational situation, revealing "the philosophy of education properly at work" in an effort "to effect a single outlook and consistent argument" (Kilpatrick, ed., 1933, p. v). All members of the committee contributed chapters to the yearbook which was issued in 1933 under the title *The Educational Frontier*. On the whole, the Yearbook reflected Dewey's experimentalist philosophy. In the introductory chapter, Boyd Bode expanded on "the movement known as 'progressive education'" and pointed out that:

the school must be transformed into a place where pupils go, not primarily to acquire knowledge, but to carry on a way of life. That is, the school is to be regarded as, first of all, an ideal community in which pupils get practice in cooperation, in self-government, and in the application of intelligence to difficulties or problems as they arise. (Bode in Kilpatrick, ed., 1933, p. 19)

In a chapter coauthored by Dewey and Childs, the practice of indoctrination in the schools in upholding laissez-faire economics and isolated nationalism was attacked as injurious to freedom of intelligence and democracy (Dewey and Childs in Kilpatrick, ed., 1933, p. 71).

According to Cremin, "If *The Educational Frontier* was the characteristic progressive statement of the decade, *The Social Frontier* was the characteristic progressive journal" (1961, p. 231). The problems addressed in *The Educational Frontier*, coupled with the deepening of the Great Depression, apparently impelled two graduate students at Teachers College, Mordecai Grossman and Norman Woelfel, to seek the establishment of a journal, *The Social Frontier*, to provide for a continued forum on the problems and issues addressed in *The Educational Frontier* (Cremin, 1988, p. 189). The first issue of *The Social Frontier* appeared in October 1934 under the editorship of George Counts with Grossman and Woelfel as associate editors. All three were to be identified among the sixty-seven founding members of the John Dewey Society. *The Social Frontier* was given its title in realization that the "geographic frontier" was closed (Counts, 1971, p. 173). The great challenge under the distressing conditions of the Great Depression was the "social frontier," and this would require that the schools serve

to prepare individuals to take part intelligently in the management of conditions under which they will live, to

bring them to an understanding of the forces which are
moving, to equip them with the intellectual and practical
tools by which they can themselves enter into direction
of these forces. (Dewey and Childs, 1933, p. 71)

Even today, one cannot pick up the issues of *The Social
Frontier* without feeling the sense of vitality and conviction
that characterized the provocative articles that addressed
the pervading issues of the time. Although Counts had
expressed the need for a more direct role of the school in
social reconstruction, and although *The Social Frontier* was
seen by many as radically progressive, its pages carried a
very broad range of opinion. And, as Cremin points out,
"*The Social Frontier* remained the only journal specifically
addressed to teachers that openly and forthrightly discussed the ideological problems of an ideological age"
(1962, p. 232).

A LOSING STRUGGLE

In tracing the short history of *The Social Frontier*, Cremin
notes that despite its fairly wide circulation, reaching some
5,000 subscribers, the magazine ran deficits so that over-
tures were made during 1937 and 1938 to have it sponsored by the Progressive Education Association. Cremin
proceeds to relate that after repeated refusals, the PEA
accepted in 1939 with the proviso that the name be changed
to *Frontiers of Democracy* under a new editorial board (pp.
232–233). Although Cremin notes that George Hartmann of
Teachers College assumed the editorship in 1937, no mention is made that the John Dewey Society had assumed
sponsorship of the magazine at that time. The ensuing ten
issues of *The Social Frontier*, volume 4 (1937–1938), carried

this caption below the masthead: *A Medium of Expression of The John Dewey Society for the Study of Education and Culture.* This may explain why some historians proceeded to cast the Society in the reconstructionist ideology. For example, after citing Counts' *Dare the School Build New Social Order?*, Adolphe Meyer described the John Dewey Society as "consecrated to the gospel of social planning" (1967, pp. 319–320). Meyer's interpretation may well have been drawn from his mistaken notion that *The Social Frontier* expressed the official position of the Dewey Society in that, "it was the organization's magazine" (p. 320) when, in actuality, the John Dewey Society sought to save The Social Frontier as it sought to save other progressive publications during desperate economic times.

With the sponsorship of *The Social Frontier* by the John Dewey Society beginning with the issue of October 1937, George W. Hartmann replaced George S. Counts as editor. Mordecai Grossman and Norman Woelfel, who had served as associate editors under Counts, continued with the magazine—with Woelfel on the Board of Editors and Grossman on the Board of Contributors. The Board of Contributors remained largely intact, with such leading figures as Charles A. Beard, Boyd H. Bode, Merle Curti, John Dewey, Joseph K. Hart, and Lewis Mumford continuing to serve. The most notable change was the appearance in every issue of "Professor Kilpatrick's Page" in place of "John Dewey's Page" which had appeared at intervals in earlier issues. Kilpatrick chaired the Board of Editors and continued to contribute articles to the magazine. "Professor Kilpatrick's Page" in the October 1937 issue pointed to the growing dangers of Japanese militarism.

Under Hartmann's editorship, and under the sponsorship of the John Dewey Society, *The Social Frontier* continued its vitality with penetrating articles from different vantage points by such contributors as Charles Beard, Norman Thomas (Socialist Party candidate for President, 1928, 1932, 1936), Bruce Bliven (editor and founder of the *New Republic)*, Henry M. Wriston (President of Brown University), Lewis Mumford, Kurt Lewin, Sidney Hook, Goodwin Watson, Will French, Earl Browder (Communist Party candidate for President, 1936), Jean Zay (French Minister of National Education), Elmer Benson (Governor of Minnesota), and Leon Trotsky. Trotsky, who was living in Mexico in exile from the Soviet Union, wrote a powerful article in *The Social Frontier* condemning Stalin for his totalitarian regime and betrayal of the Russian people (April, 1938, pp. 211–214). Two years later, Trotsky was assassinated in Mexico on Stalin's orders. I. I. Rabi, the Nobel Laureate in physics, contributed to the Book Review section of the magazine.

With its tiny but active membership, the John Dewey Society's treasury was very modest and could not possibly continue to meet the deficits of *The Social Frontier* while also meeting the demands of its expanding publications program. In an editorial in the PEA's magazine *Progressive Education* (April, 1939), W. Carson Ryan, President of the PEA, alluded to the arrangement for the PEA to sponsor *The Social Frontier's* successor *(Frontiers of Democracy)*. "One of the present efforts to make education count more than it has for democracy," wrote Ryan, "takes the form of a plan for coordinating the social and educational forces represented in the Progressive Education Association, the John Dewey Society, and *The Social Frontier*" (p. 226).

However, *Frontiers of Democracy* was to become a mere shadow of *The Social Frontier*. In the last issue of *Frontiers of Democracy* (December 15, 1943), editor Harold Rugg wrote a lengthy and bitter editorial in which he raised questions concerning the commitment of the PEA to its professed principles. Ironically, with the demise of the Progressive Education Association twelve years later, the John Dewey Society was to fight a losing struggle to continue the publication of *Progressive Education.*

The SOCIAL FRONTIER

A journal of educational criticism and reconstruction

A MEDIUM OF EXPRESSION OF THE JOHN DEWEY SOCIETY FOR THE STUDY OF EDUCATION AND CULTURE

Volume IV   OCTOBER, 1937   Number 28

Contents

Contents of previous issues of THE SOCIAL FRONTIER may be found by consulting the Education Index

The Changing Scene

❡ *EVIDENTLY SOMETHING LIKE AN EDU-*
cational renaissance is occurring in Pennsylvania if the report which Dr. Lester K. Ade, the Superintendent of Public Instruction, has sent us is a proper indication. A total of 455 educational bills were introduced in 1937 and 141 passed the legislature. Improved teacher tenure conditions, recreational and social opportunities for out-of-school youth, county supervisors of special education (actually, travelling clinical psychologists), and a substantial building program for state institutions, are some of the advances insured by recent measures. In his comment, Dr. Ade notes, "These liberal measures, in tune with today's trends, reflect the new era of our democracy. They bear irrefutable testimony that the people of Pennsylvania are searching for new horizons on their social, industrial and educational frontiers. . . . The function of public education goes further than keeping pace with evolving civilization; it must interpret to youth the deeper implications of these changes, and *exert some influence on directing social trends*" (our italics). Although a bit skeptical of the degree to which these brave words (they might have come from the Editors of this journal!) accord with the actual conditions of most Pennsylvania schools, we hail them as a sign that a new climate of opinion is emerging in that great commonwealth.

❡ *THE SOCIAL FRONTIER IS NOTORIOUS-*
ly not a conservative sheet, but it gladly opens its columns to any conservative who wants to express dissent from our brand of socialized progressivism. For this reason we are happy to juxtapose the antithetical papers of President Wriston and Dr. Harding on the Supreme Court question. This issue, though temporarily shelved, cuts as deeply into the fabric of American life as any current problem, and

IX

THE JOHN DEWEY SOCIETY AND THE PROGRESSIVE EDUCATION ASSOCIATION

... given the present crisis and hysteria with its attendant fears and tendencies to run for cover ...

THE PROPOSED MERGER

The year 1940 proved to be a decisive one for the John Dewey Society. During the previous two years, some of the members had indicated that they favored a merger with the Progressive Education Association. The matter was taken up at the business session of the annual meeting of the Society in St. Louis on February 25, 1940. The small group in attendance at the business session overwhelmingly rejected the proposed merger. However, it was understood that the entire membership of the Society would be polled on the proposal. A letter from Jesse Newlon dated July 19, 1940 and addressed to William Kilpatrick, who was then a visiting professor in the School of Education at Northwestern University, expressed Newlon's concern about proceeding with plans for a forthcoming yearbook for the Society before the outcome of the polling of the membership for merger with the PEA. In his letter, Newlon also mentioned the inaccurate press given to an address he had delivered at Teachers College the previous week revealing "some malice towards the liberal group at Teachers College. However, the favorable response to this address from all sorts of people, has been truly astonishing," added Newlon. Kilpatrick's reply of July 29 reported that he was attempting to obtain statements pro and con regarding the proposed merger of the Society with the Progressive Education Association to be submitted to the Society's members along with a ballot. On December 20, 1940 unsigned statements for and against the merger were sent to the membership along with a cover letter from Kilpatrick and a ballot. The statement "In Favor of the Merger" held that merger with the PEA, NEA, or AFT would enable the Society to conduct research on a national scale and provide for greater contact with teachers and the schools to develop programs based upon the research findings. "In these days of economies, it is not only difficult but next to impossible to set up another national association with machinery for implementation," declared the statement in reference to the implementation of a national research program.

The statement "In Opposition to the Merger" held that the continued existence of the John Dewey Society "(small and weak though it may be)" serves to bring "liberally-minded and socially-conscious educators . . . to work with others of similar outlook and interest." A major portion of the opposition statement is quoted below in that it reveals the PEA membership as sharing a "reformed psychological outlook" but lacking a unified "socio-economic-political outlook," as compared with the more unified and wider social consciousness of the members of the John Dewey Society. The reference to the shared "reformed *psychological* outlook" of the PEA apparently points to the child-centered pedagogy in humanizing the progressive private and public schools while avoiding the unpleasantries of a curriculum directed at pervading social problems and issues. The opposition statement goes on to express concern that the large proportion of PEA members, having no abiding interest in a shared social outlook, would be unwilling and unable to face up to conditions of crisis and attack—as indicated by the present situation of "hysteria with its attendant fears and tendencies to run to cover."

> The present relatively large membership of the PEA includes a great many individuals who are not particularly interested in or concerned about the reciprocal relationship between the school and culture. As these members succeed in electing representatives of like mind to the governing board of the PEA, the present attention now given to this relationship by the John Dewey Society group would to that degree be diluted were this group subsumed within the larger PEA entity. In time (and at a time not so far distant, given the present crisis and hysteria with its attendant fears and tendencies to run for cover) it might conceivably thus come to engage but a very negligibly minor portion of the interests, efforts, and funds of the governing or executive group. Although the PEA membership is not an unselected lot, the PEA has primarily tended to screen together those educators possessed of a reformed *psychological* outlook. . . . Though much more rather than less of one common psychological outlook, the PEA membership is not in any particularly appreciable sense a unitary group with reference to socio-economic-political outlook. The John Dewey Society membership to a considerably greater degree represents some such unity of point of view.

The outcome of the vote, as revealed in a letter to Kilpatrick dated January 14, 1941 and signed by Jesse Newlon and Donald Cottrell, was the rejection of the proposed merger with the PEA by the narrowest of margins. Only 103 ballots were returned, with fifty-two opposed and forty-nine in favor of the merger.

With only a few hundred members, the John Dewey Society was indeed miniscule in comparison to the PEA's membership of some 10,000. Yet history was to deal unkindly with the PEA. As indicated in the statement in opposition to the merger of the Dewey Society with the PEA, progressive educators were coming under increasing attacks and the PEA membership was too diffuse to answer the attacks. As Cremin relates, "the year 1940 was something of an open season on progressive teachers, as national magazines . . . lashed out against the movement as naively sentimental on the one hand, dangerously subversive on the other" (1961, p. 267). In the absence of a platform to define its mission, the PEA had appointed a Committee on Philosophy of Education in 1938. The Committee's report, issued under the chairmanship of Harold Alberty of Ohio State as a special supplement to *Progressive Education* in May, 1941, is described by Cremin as "Deweyan from beginning to end" and as "the most fundamental statement of principles ever to issue from the PEA." However, the report was never formally adopted by the Association (1961, pp. 266–267).

A notable strategy of the leadership of the John Dewey Society from the very birth of the organization was to hold the Society's meetings in conjunction with the annual meetings of much larger educational groups. Hence in February of 1941, the Dewey Society conducted well-attended sessions at the annual meeting of the Progressive Education Association in Philadelphia and the American Association of School Administrators in Atlantic City. The sessions sponsored by the Dewey Society at both meetings featured the Society's fifth yearbook, *Worker's Education in the United States* (1941), under the editorship of Theodore Brameld of the University of Minnesota.

The matter of merger of the John Dewey Society was raised once again after World War II on the floor of the Society's annual meeting in Atlantic City in March of 1947. John C. Robertson of Temple University proposed that the Society merge with the American Education Fellowship, the new name adopted by the Progressive Education Association in the spring of 1944. However, the proposal gained insufficient support to bring it before a vote of the entire membership. At the meeting of the Society's Executive Board held at the Bureau of Intercultural Education in New York City on April 2526, 1947 and chaired by Ernest O. Melby of Northwestern University, President of the Society, the matter of cooperation or affiliation with other organizations, specifically the American Education Fellowship, was raised. It was voted on a motion by Harold Benjamin of the University of Colorado that "the Society will cooperate with any organization or group on matters of mutual concern, but will merge with none."

THE JOHN DEWEY SOCIETY AND THE AMERICAN EDUCATION FELLOWSHIP

The minutes of the Board meeting of November 22–23, 1948 report on the possibility of a jointly sponsored series of pamphlets with the American Education Fellowship. In a lengthy memo to the Society's Board dated January 20, 1949, H. Gordon Hullfish reported on his meeting with John J. DeBoer, President of the AEF, and others at the University of Illinois to discuss the prospects for the pamphlet series. Hullfish stated that he had presented to the AEF group the prefatory statement for each pamphlet in the series, as approved by the Dewey Society's Board at its November meeting the previous year. Hullfish reported that the AEF group was willing to include the prefatory statement in each pamphlet of the series. The statement included the following propositions, revealing the Society's dedication to an open spirit of discourse along with concern that the AEF leadership should not assume a doctrinaire stance in the pamphlet series:

- each serious and responsible voice in the profession has a right to be heard
- shared thinking will lead men progressively to more intelligent and humane action
- no view that holds itself to be above criticism is a proper ground on which to construct a democratic education

Manuscripts for two pamphlets were ready for publication—one by Kilpatrick and one by a committee of the AEF chaired by Willard B. Spalding. (The latter, *Organizing for Teacher Welfare,* had taken a militant stance for teachers' unionization and was considered to be particularly controversial.) Despite these notable efforts, a pamphlet series, as originally conceived, never materialized.

In connection with the proposed joint pamphlets project, the minutes of November 22–23, 1948 reveal that the Board devoted some discussion to what appeared to be internal disagreement in the American Education Fellowship:

It was reported that a left-wing faction was considering independent action either within the organization or as a separate agency. Theodore Brameld, who was reported to be active in this movement, was asked to discuss the movement with the Board. It was learned that the movement apparently had not made much progress and that the issue at stake was primarily one of how much emphasis should be given by the profession to social action.

In light of this discussion it was later argued that the Society's annual meeting should be devoted to an exploration of how the liberal forces in education might be united into a strong spearhead organization reminiscent of the Progressive Education Association at its best. There was some hope expressed that the AEF might come out publicly as a noncommunist organization, if urged to do so, thereby clarifying the situation preparatory to building it into the desired spearheading agency.

The reference to the need for a noncommunist declaration signifies just how far the Cold War era of suspicion and hysteria had gone. Although Cremin (1961) makes no mention of such suspicions surrounding the American Education Fellowship, it should be noted that John DeBoer of the University of Illinois, President of the AEF at the time, was among a group of Marxists growing out of the Great Depression who were critical of experimentalist theory. As Cremin states,

> Some who were Marxist critics during the 1930s—Theodore Brameld is a case in point—moved into the liberal camp during the 1940s and 1950s; others—one thinks of John DeBoer at the University of Illinois—maintained their position in lonely isolation. (1988, p. 195)

Nevertheless, the American Education Fellowship (or the PEA) never acted to implement a unified program for socio-political-educational action based upon a reconstructionist orientation, let alone a Marxist orientation.

Cremin comments that *The Social Frontier* was commonly charged with being subject to communist influence, and Cremin sees this allegation as "somewhat ridiculous" (1961, p. 234). If such charges against *The Social Frontier* were ridiculous, then surely they were even more ridiculous in connection with the American Education Fellowship, which had a highly diverse membership and never assumed a radical platform. As noted in the minutes of the Dewey Society Board meeting of November 22–23, Theodore Brameld, who was active in a so-called leftist faction in the AEF, had reported that it had not made much progress and that separation from the AEF was being considered. The issue at stake, as noted in the minutes, rested on the extent to which the AEF should be committed to promoting social action on the part of the education profession. This issue reflected the remnants of the reconstructionist-experimentalist debate which had grown out of the Great Depression, and was in no way connected with communism or communist influence in the AEF.

Nevertheless, the concern about the "leftist faction" in the AEF, coupled with the concern about survival of the AEF, impelled William Kilpatrick to write to William O. Stanley of the University of Illinois on December 15, 1948. In the letter, Kilpatrick refers to a meeting in New York of some members of the John Dewey Society concerned about the viability of the American Education Fellowship. A notation at the top of the letter, apparently in Kilpatrick's handwriting, indicates that the meeting took place on December 13 in the office of George Counts. Kilpatrick's letter does not identify the members of the Dewey Society group who had initiated the inquiry. A telegram sent to Kilpatrick on January 19, 1949 from William O. Stanley indicates a favorable response by the Illinois group to Kilpatrick's inquiry and that a letter had been sent to Kilpatrick. The telegram bears the following notation, apparently in Kilpatrick's handwriting: "WHK to Dr. Thut, Dr. Thut to Dean Melby, Dean Melby to Professors Counts & Childs, finally back to

WHK." This notation appears to identify the Dewey Society group who had initiated the inquiry.

Kilpatrick's letter inquires as to what the John Dewey Society might do to help the AEF "get back on its feet so as to regain the prestige and influence the Progressive Education Association formerly held in American education." In the letter, Kilpatrick asks Stanley to get the opinion of others at the University of Illinois where the AEF leadership was now located without necessarily revealing Kilpatrick's inquiry on the part of the Dewey Society group, and to make a personal assessment of these opinions as to whether it is too late to save the AEF and wiser to start a new spearhead organization on behalf of "better modern education" (apparently a euphemism for progressive education). The letter assures Stanley that his response will be treated in confidence. The letter asks whether the present AEF officers would cooperate on rebuilding the organization. Here Kilpatrick adds that he recalls that John DeBoer is inclined to resign and allow a new leadership to take charge. Then Kilpatrick asks, "Would it not be wise to adopt a specific article of the constitution to the effect that no member of the Communist Party is to be admitted to membership of the organization?"

Obviously, DeBoer's presidency of the AEF was considered by the Dewey Society group to be a liability. But neither DeBoer's presidency nor the so-called "left-wing faction" in the AEF could be connected with the decline of the AEF. The organization was faced with sharply declining membership and influence when it changed its name from the Progressive Education Association to the American Education Fellowship back in 1944, well before DeBoer's presidency.

Finally Kilpatrick's letter asks for an opinion on the question of restoring the old name, the Progressive Education Association, and whether the Illinois group would agree to have the organization "count the psychological learning process aspect and social improvement aspect as both essential to the democratic program to be advocated." Here Kilpatrick appears to have been alluding to the strong social stance for which the AEF leadership was identified and his view that the organization should soften its image by addressing the teaching-learning process, as was the case with the organization at its peak of membership and influence. This was indeed an ironic twist, for the PEA had been criticized years earlier for lacking a strong social outlook. Significantly, the policy statement adopted by the AEF back in 1944 was focused on promoting both progressive educational reform and social reform, including "democratic civic practices that will do away with religious and racial intolerance" (Board of Directors, American Education Fellowship, 1944–1945). Nevertheless, the AEF never launched a concerted program linking educational reform with social reform.

The reply by William O. Stanley dated January 29, 1949 reveals that Stanley's earlier response was never received by Kilpatrick. In his detailed letter, Stanley stated that after a meeting of the Illinois group and a good many conversations, he was able to report that the group was pleased that the John Dewey Society Board has taken an interest in the AEF, and that the unanimous opinion was that they should try to rebuild the prestige of the AEF—"a going organization with a long and honored history."

Acknowledging that "the AEF has made some enemies and (that) both the war and the recent controversies had weakened it," Stanley stated that the organization "has

assets among the teachers of America that no new organization could achieve for many years." Stanley's reply
states that the Illinois group was all in favor of readopt-
ing the original name of the organization, that they saw
no problem in embracing the wider program as identified
in Kilpatrick's letter, but that they opposed any effort to
retreat from the AEF's commitment to social improvement.

On the question of the AEF's adoption of a constitutional clause denying membership to anyone who holds
membership in the Communist Party, Stanley reported that
the group was unable to agree on such a clause in that (1)
the AEF clearly stands for democracy and democratic education, and is opposed to all forms of totalitarianism and
undemocratic beliefs and practices, (2) there is no problem
of communist penetration in the AEF, (3) if communists are
to be barred from membership, then all outright totalitarian groups should likewise be barred, and (4) such a membership test would be ineffective since communists "will
sign anything if it suits their purpose while some liberals
seem to resent such tests on principle." Finally, Stanley's
letter points out that such a disallowing clause in the AEF
constitution "would be tantamount to a rebuke to them
(liberals) for having participated in the Wallace movement,
and to an invitation for them to withdraw from the AEF if
in the future they participated in such movements."

The mention of the "Wallace movement" was in reference to the candidacy of Henry A. Wallace for U.S. President on the Progressive Party ticket in 1948. Wallace, who
had served as U.S. Vice President from 1941 to 1945 under
Franklin Roosevelt, had refused on principle to disavow
communist support of the Progressive Party with disastrous results for the campaign. Clearly not a communist,
Wallace and his campaign were badly smeared by his

political opposition and the media. The Progressive Party had attracted many liberals who, with Wallace, were concerned about the "saber rattling" of the Cold War in a nuclear age. The principle against "disavowal" also came to be related to the Truman Loyalty Order of 1947, requiring federal employees to submit to a loyalty investigation so as to deny employment to anyone holding membership or in sympathetic association with any organization adjudged by the Attorney General to be communist, totalitarian, or subversive. The federal Loyalty Order was followed by the widespread requirement of teacher loyalty oaths by the states. A number of liberals who refused to sign such an oath on principle were removed from their teaching positions in publicly supported colleges, universities, and schools. Ironically the first formal meeting of the John Dewey Society, held in St. Louis on February 23, 1936, was devoted to the topic, "Teachers' Loyalty Oaths—Fascism?" The session which vigorously criticized teacher loyalty oaths was chaired by William Kilpatrick.

Kilpatrick's letter to William O. Stanley is reproduced in its entirety along with Stanley's extended reply in that they reveal the significant relationship that existed between the John Dewey Society and the AEF—a relationship that years later was to find the Dewey Society making a valiant but failed effort to save the journal *Progressive Education* following the demise of the renamed Progressive Education Association.

TEACHERS COLLEGE
Columbia University

Dec. 15, 1948

Professor William O. Stanley
College of Education
University of Illinois
Urbana, Ill.

Dear Dr. Stanley:

Several of us here in New York are concerned as to what the John Dewey Society should and can do to help the A.E.F. get back on its feet so as to regain the prestige and influence the Progressive Education Association formerly held in American education. As we have talked together it has seemed to us that you and your colleagues of the University of Illinois are in a position to advise us. It was accordingly agreed that I should ask you for your personal opinion of the situation.

We should be glad for you to talk with others of your group, saying as little about us as you think wise, and report what *you* personally think *they* think about the following questions:

1. Is it too late to do anything with the A.E.F.? Should the friends of better modern education unite to start a new spear-head organization?

2. If it seems wise (as I myself think) to work on, and for, the A.E.F., will the present officers cooperate? (I seem to recall that DeBoer is inclined to resign and let a new administration tackle the problem.)

3. What would you think of restoring the old name, The Progressive Education Association?

4. Can agreement be secured to count the psychological learning process aspect and the social improvement aspect as both essential to the democratic program to be advocated?

5. Would it not be wise to adopt a specific article of the constitution to the effect that no member of the Communist Party is to be admitted to membership in the organization?

If you will write me fully on these points, we shall appreciate it. I may add that your name will be carefully safeguarded. We have no wish to quote you, but merely to say that "we believe we are reliably informed that the University of Illinois group think thus and so"; and we have every wish to avoid adding to any present feelings of opposition or distrust anywhere existing.

Sincerely yours,

/S/ William H. Kilpatrick

UNIVERSITY OF ILLINOIS
COLLEGE OF EDUCATION
URBANA

January 29, 1949

Professor William H. Kilpatrick
106 Morningside Drive
New York 27, New York

Dear Professor Kilpatrick:

I am very sorry that you and the John Dewey Society Board were inconvenienced by the failure of my letter to reach you. I can not imagine what has happened to it. Since receiving your last letter I have been involved in examinations and a four day conference.

After one meeting and a good many conversations I would say that opinion on the Illinois campus with respect to the questions raised in your letter of December 15 is as follows:

1. Without exception we are glad that the John Dewey Society Board has taken an interest in the problem.

2. Again without exception we feel that it is definitely worth while to try to rebuild the prestige and influence of the

A.E.F. A going organization with a long and honored history is nearly always a better base of operations than a new organization unless the latter has unusually strong financial backing. The A.E.F. has made some enemies and both the war and the recent controversaries have temporarily weakened it. But it has assets among the teachers of America that no new organization could achieve for many years. Financially the A.E.F. has an income of nearly $20,000 per year which can be greatly increased if its friends again become active in its behalf. As you know some rather heavy debts have accumulated in the last few years. But since moving the office to Champaign the organization has met its current bills and has begun substantial repayment on the debt. In a few days the A.E.F. will receive about $3,200 from a bequest which will still further reduce the debt. If we want a liberal spearhead organization in education it seems to us that it would be short sighted to liquidate the A.E.F. in favor of another organization. On the other hand it is true that the A.E.F. cannot do much more than publish a magazine and a few pamphlets until it has more income.

3. So far as the projected meeting in New York is concerned the A.E. F. officers on this campus will give it strong personal support. If any significant agreement is reached at the meeting it would, in any event, require registration through official A.E.F. machinery involving many persons not on the Illinois campus. Our entire group, including Professors DeBoer and Smith, would welcome any move that would strengthen the A.E.F. Mr. DeBoer's term of office expires in February, and he intends to serve only until his successor is elected. At the present time, I understand, Professor Benne is the only candidate for the presidency on the ballot, the other three persons named by the nominating committee having withdrawn their names.

4. The sentiment here is all in favor of returning to the old name as fast as possible. Those of us that were not out of the country at the time the name was changed were opposed to the change, and feel that time has vindicated our original position.

5. From our stand point there should be no difficulty about an agreement to count the psychological and social aspects as both essential to the democratic program to be

advocated. As we understand it that is the present policy. But if there is any doubt about the matter we would favor any statement that would clarify the situation. We would, however, oppose any effort to weaken or withdraw the commitment to the social improvement aspect.

6. No clear cut and unanimous agreement could be reached here with respect to all of the issues raised by the question bearing on a constitutional clause disqualifying members of the Communist Party for membership in the A.E.F. We were able to agree on the following points:

a. The A.E.F. stands for, and (if it has not already done so) should make it clear that it stands for, a democratic program designed to advance the cause of democracy in the school, the nation and the world. This means that the A.E.F. is opposed to all forms of totalitarianism, and to all types of undemocratic beliefs and practices.

b. There is, so far as we can see, no problem of actual communist penetration into the A.E.F.

c. The nature of the communist movement, coupled with the fact that the A.E.F. membership is scattered throughout the nation would, except for a few avowed communists, make a non-communist clause in the constitution largely a matter of public relations rather than an effective way of keeping communists out of the organization.

d. We doubt that it would be wise to impose any membership test or to attempt to bring suspects to trial. A membership test would actually operate to screen out some non-communists rather than communists since the latter will sign anything if it suits their purpose while some liberals seem to resent such tests on principle.

e. If it is decided to bar communists from membership, then it should be done on the ground that they fundamentally reject the democratic purposes of the A.E.F. This ground would seem to indicate that the exclusion should extend to members of all out-right totalitarian groups, fascist as well as communists. From this point on the group here could not fully agree. Many of us were willing to support the constitutional provision suggested in your letter although most of this group would also be content with a clearcut statement that the A.E.F. is opposed to all forms of totalitarianism, specifically including the communists and fascists by name.

A smaller group tended to oppose the constitutional prohibition, while accepting the declaration of opposition to totalitarianism. But they would not agree to a specific mention of communism and fascism unless all other kinds of undemocratic groups were also mentioned—obviously an impossible task.

Personally I believe that if care is used in framing the statement both of these two groups, at least as they are represented on this campus, can reach an agreement on this issue. No one believes that A.E.F. should be permitted to become a communist front or that it should enter into any kind of united front with the communists. Hence there is no substantive issue so far as the A.E.F. is concerned. But some of our people do feel that, as persons, they should work with communists on certain issues in other connections. What they are really reacting to is an inference which I do not draw, namely that a no-communist clause in the A.E.F. constitution would be tantamount to a rebuke to them for having participated in the Wallace movement, and to an invitation to them to withdraw from the A.E.F. if in the future they participate in such movements. If this implication can be avoided it might well be possible to heal the breach in the two wings of the liberal camp so far as the A.E.F. is concerned. I may add that most of us here feel that it is important that, in some way, the A.E.F. make its position entirely clear. Perhaps the formula used by the A.V.C. might be helpful in framing such a statement.

Please allow me to state again that all of us here feel that some such move as that comtemplated by the John Dewey Society Board is badly needed and that it offers considerable hope of achieving some very desirable results.

Cordially yours,

William Stanley

W. O. Stanley
Assistant Professor of Education

WOS:s

X

THE PROBLEM OF PURPOSE
IN THE POSTWAR PERIOD

... most of the problems on the 'cutting edge' of society and education are dangerous problems.
—Archibald W. Anderson

The meeting of the Society's Executive Board on April
25–26, 1947 was devoted mainly to detailed discussion
concerning the purposes and functions of the John Dewey
Society, including its publications program and the need to
build up the membership matters that had been given consideration at the meetings of the Board the previous year.
(During the years of World War II the membership had
declined and the activities of the Society were curtailed—
although the Society continued to issue notable yearbooks.)
Extensive memorandums for discussion of these concerns
at the April, 1947 meetings of the Board were prepared by
Archibald Anderson, William F. Bruce, Hollis L. Caswell,
C. L. Cushman, I. M. Thut, and William Van Til.

SEEKING WAYS TO STRENGTHEN FORCES
THAT ARE WORKING FOR DEMOCRACY

The minutes of the meeting of the Executive Board on
April 25–26, 1947 reported that although the Board was
not willing to think of the Society as an "action" group,

"the Society should build a place for itself on the educational scene by initiating desirable projects and studies." In this connection, the Board identified the need to address "the low state to which faith in the democratic process had fallen." The statement continued as follows:

> We need to think about democracy, and to interpret the way or ways in which the loss of faith has come about. We should, however, adopt a positive approach to the problem, seeking ways to strengthen the forces that are working for democracy, rather than to focus attention upon the forces that are opposing it. We should emphasize and interpret the meaning of democracy, publicize it, and work for its more widespread application in the educative process. A reexamination of the meaning of democracy for the community, for public administration including the schools, for intercultural and international relations, for economics, for religion, and for the science of education are part of the total problem.

A summary statement added to the Board minutes of April 25–26 identified the role of the Society as "bolstering faith in democracy and the democratic process," and the scope of the Society's work as to (1) "encourage and, when necessary, initiate and support basic studies in the field of educational theory and in fields that affect educational theory" (2), "exercise leadership in the interpretation of theory and data in terms of their meaning for schools and society," and (3) "engage in whatever activities are necessary to communicate its ideas to the professional and lay groups in order that such ideas may be translated into practice." The statement reiterated the Board's decision that "the Society should cooperate with any agency or organization that is willing to work toward democratic ends, but should merge with none."

INVOLVEMENT OF EDUCATORS AT ALL LEVELS

The above statements and actions of the Board were made following extended discussion of the memorandums prepared in advance of the meetings of April 25–26 by individual Board members. A two-page memorandum by Hollis Caswell contained the following recommendation concerning the critical issues to be addressed by the Society and the kinds of persons who should be called upon to address these issues:

> I believe that the Society should deal primarily with current critical issues in education in terms of their social and philosophical bases. At the present time questions such as the following might be made the subject of study:
>
> (1) Avenues of organized action by the teaching profession.
>
> (2) Separation of church and state as it relates to education.
>
> (3) Discrimination in education.
>
> (4) Defining the teacher's professional responsibilities.
> I believe that the Society should seek to interest workers in all aspects of education. It should include professors in teacher training institutions from all fields, administrators, curriculum directors, supervisors, and classroom teachers. The test should be interest in dealing with the fundamental aspects of currently critical problems. There should be a deliberate effort, I think, to get representation from all of the major groups in the educational field.

Caswell not only had identified some of the most critical problems facing education, but he viewed the Society as being necessarily engaged with educators at all levels. Caswell's views clearly meshed with those of Henry Harap and those who had been involved in the initial chain of events that led to the founding of the Society. It will be recalled that Harap's letter of January 3, 1934 was addressed to Paul Hanna with the request that Hanna persuade Jesse Newlon to convene the first meeting of what was to become the John Dewey Society. Harap, Hanna, and Newlon were noted curricularists. As noted earlier, the sixty-seven founding members of the Society were to be representative of persons engaged at all levels of education, rather than those whose professional work was directed primarily at educational philosophy or theory.

Significantly, the Society's yearbooks were anything but limited to educational theory. From the time of the issuance of the first yearbook in 1937 to the meeting of the Executive Board in 1947, the yearbooks were devoted to wide-ranging themes encompassing teacher education, the curriculum, academic freedom, workers' education, mobilizing educational resources for winning the war and the peace, the high school, and so on—all related to the role and function of the schools in a democratic society. Indeed the yearbooks were to continue in this broad stream until the last yearbook (1963), *Negro Education in America.*

UNIQUE ROLE OF THE JOHN DEWEY SOCIETY

From the time of its inception, the John Dewey Society had addressed the widest and deepest concerns interfacing school and society without being wedded to a doctrinaire line. Indeed the Society's work was in a Deweyan tradition. In his memorandum prepared for the Board meeting of April 25–26, 1947, Archibald Anderson pointed to the essential difference between the John Dewey Society and the Philosophy of Education Society. The Philosophy of Education Society was composed of members representing vastly divergent philosophical systems, and there are many organizations concerned with the implementation of educational theory, Anderson pointed out. However, stressed Anderson, "the John Dewey Society is the only organization which has been devoted to a study of the relationship of school and society in the light of a pragmatic democratic philosophy." Anderson's memorandum went on to define the role of the John Dewey Society as devoted to the exploration of fundamental issues "on the educational and social frontier" in the light of such a philosophy, but the Society should not become directly engaged in the implementation of programmatic reform in school and society.

Although Caswell had never viewed the Society's role as directly activist, he envisioned the Society as being properly engaged in the study of educational problems beyond the scope of the interests of university professors, particularly those whose specialty was educational theory. Here Caswell had differed with Anderson who viewed the Society as devoted to the study of educational theory and that it be promoted in the light of "pragmatic democratic philosophy." In Anderson's words:

> Implicit in the exploration of these issues is a continuing exploration of the educational philosophy and educational theory of democracy as it is applied to problems on the educational and social frontier and as it is refined, expanded, and clarified in the process of such application.
>
> Although no exploration of pragmatic theory can ignore the implications of theory for practice, I do not think that the implementation of theory is either a responsibility or a direct concern of the John Dewey Society. The Society's responsibility for implementation will be discharged if it persistently strives to bring to the attention of professional organizations concerned with implementation of the results of the Society's exploration

of the social and educational frontier, and if it consistently subjects to criticism the programs of professional 'organizations concerned With implementation. The John Dewey Society can fulfill this function by working cooperatively with other professional organizations rather than by affiliating with any one such organization or by diffusing its efforts by itself adopting a program of implementation.

The memorandum by William Van Til of the University of Illinois was focused on the need for the Society to communicate to the public and to classroom teachers "the great needs of American experimental education."

PROBLEMS: PERVASIVE AND "DANGEROUS"

The minutes of the Board meeting of April 25–26, 1947, do not reveal the nature of the discussions that took place concerning the differences in views as expressed in the memorandums, but instead identified the points of agreement on the role of the Society—as noted earlier. Several of the memorandums, including the one by Archibald Anderson, called for the expansion of the Society's publications program, including the launching of a journal devoted to pervasive problems and issues on the educational and social frontier. Acknowledging the difficulties of such a venture in consideration of the Society's limited finances and modest size, Anderson reported that he had received a proposal calling for the Society's support of *Progressive Education*, the journal of the American Education Fellowship (formerly the Progressive Education Association), with a separate section in the journal specifically designated for the John Dewey Society. However, Anderson indicated that there were arguments for and against the proposal that required investigation. (Almost ten years were to pass before the John Dewey Society was to assume the publication of *Progressive Education* following the demise of the journal's parent organization.)

Whereas most of the memorandums pointed to the need for the Society to build its membership, Anderson contended that the number of persons interested in concentrated theoretical study not only is small, but that "most of the problems on the 'cutting edge' of society and education are 'dangerous problems.'" Here Anderson was referring to the danger faced by school personnel in affiliating with a progressive organization or in expressing ideas in a publication of a progressive association. Indeed the late 1940s were witnessing the rise of organized right-wing groups that were attacking the public schools as seedbeds of progressive or "subversive" ideas. Under the circumstances, Anderson probably was not exaggerating when he wrote that, "Only courageous individuals or individuals with some degree of security in their jobs can afford to have their name associated with an organization which stirs up prejudices by examining fundamental issues." The implication, continued Anderson, "is that membership in the Society should be limited to those who are willing to accept the hazards of the kind of fundamental exploration for which the Society stands."

TOO CONTROVERSIAL FOR THE
SCHOOL ADMINISTRATORS

Turning to the matter concerning future meetings of the Society, Anderson expressed his view in favor of holding the annual meeting at the time of the annual meeting of the American Association of School Administrators, and of holding joint meetings with such organizations as the American Education Fellowship and the Association for Supervision and Curriculum Development "providing that safeguards be set up so that the Society be something more than a mere appendage, with its own theoretical emphasis engulfed in the clamor for a program of 'practical action.'"

Nevertheless, the Society's forums at the annual meetings of the American Association of School Administrators were hardly devoted to esoteric theorizing. On the contrary, they were directed at the open examination of penetrating problems and controversial issues. As fate would have it, the Dewey Society program proved to be too controversial for the school administrators. The minutes of the meeting of the Society's Executive Board on November 10–11, 1947 in New York City, reveal that the Society was refused accommodation at the February, 1947 annual meeting of the American Association of School Administrators in Atlantic City. The minutes do not reveal the reasons for such refusal, but simply report on discussions concerning possible locales for the Society's 1948 meeting. William Van Til, who was a member of the Executive Board of the Society and who was present at the Board's meeting on November 10–11, 1947, recounts that the annual meetings of the Society held at the convention of the American Association of School Administrators in Atlantic City were so lively that they had gained some notoriety. Charles A. Beard's attack on the William Randolph Hearst press at one such meeting of the Society caused the Hearst press to rage and the school superintendents to panic, according to Van Til (1983, p. 189).

Unwelcome at the 1948 meeting of AASA, the minutes of the John Dewey Society's Board meeting of November 10–11, 1947 reveal that consideration was given to holding the Society's 1948 meeting in Philadelphia immediately following the annual meeting of the Philosophy of Education Society. However, the Dewey Society proceeded to hold its annual meetings in Atlantic City over the next several years independent of any organization until the Society was to begin a long-term arrangement to meet at the annual meeting of the American Association of Colleges for Teacher Education in Chicago.

The heightened attacks against the schools during the postwar years found the Executive Board considering the possibility of participating in arranging an "'Off Record' Conference on Attacks on Education" involving representation from thirteen professional educational associations, the Educational Policies Commission, several education journals, and the American Booksellers Association. The documents relating to the proposed conference are undated. A letter proposing such a conference, signed by a Richard Barnes Kennan, is addressed to I. N. Thut, Executive Secretary of the Society. The letter is undated and bears no letterhead. A list of prospective organizations and educational publications to be represented at the proposed conference includes *Building America* which, it will be recalled, ended publication in 1948. Consequently, the plans for the conference probably were being conceived around that time or a year or so earlier. An undated and unsigned document canvassing the membership on the possible sites for the conference notes that of the sites being considered (Buck Hill Falls, Pennsylvania, Baltimore, Wilmington, Harpers Ferry, and Atlantic City) only Atlantic City and Buck Hill

Falls would be feasible "if there are likely to be Negro dele-
gates." Whether such a conference was ever held, and what
role was played by the Dewey Society in such a conference,
could not be determined from the incomplete sets of minutes of the Executive Board meetings during the postwar
period.

RENEWAL OF PURPOSE

The postwar period of reconstruction had given urgency
for the leadership of the John Dewey Society to take stock
of its founding mission and vision. At a time of Cold War
hysteria and heightened attacks on the public schools, the
question was whether the Society should retreat into the
safe haven of educational theory and become another philosophical society in academia, or whether it should renew
its active commitment to the advancement of the democratic prospect for school and society. Here Hollis Caswell
contended that the Dewey Society must address the critical
issues, including racial discrimination, the professionalization of teaching, curriculum development for democratic
life, and academic freedom. Caswell and his allies were to
win out as evidenced by the character and impact of the
Society's yearbooks and activities in upholding academic
freedom. This was no easy task. In fact the Society was to
lose many battles—notably to the censors of the Building
America texts who viewed any recognition and study of
social problems in the school curriculum as subversive to
the national interest. Nevertheless, the question remained
as to whether the Society would continue to stand up and
hold fast to its founding purpose in the years to come, or
whether it would evolve or erode into another purely, or
almost purely, academic society.

XI

NEW DIRECTIONS

... organized attacks on the achievements of progressive education have become more extensive and virulent than ever before.

—John Dewey

In a letter addressed to the membership on March 19, 1947, I. N. Thut, Secretary-Treasurer, reported that at the Society's annual meeting in Atlantic City on March 2 and 4, it was decided that the Society would "merge with the group of younger men who are conducting an editorial writing project in *Educational Administration and Supervision* under the heading of 'By Way of Comment.'" The use of the term "merge" is baffling since the Society's Board minutes of April 25–26, 1947, along with the various memorandums prepared for discussion on those dates, simply endorse the continuation and expansion of the "By Way of Comment Section" in *Educational Administration and Supervision* as part of the Society's effort to communicate to a wider audience the need to uphold American democratic educational traditions.

The journal, *Educational Administration and Supervision*, had been in continuous publication since 1916 and its contributors over the years included many of the leading figures in education, addressing the widest range of concerns in educational administration, supervision, curriculum, and teacher education. The journal was edited by H. E. Bucholz in association with Harold B. Alberty, Archibald W. Anderson, Boyd H. Bode, William F. Bruce, Ernest O. Melby, and I. N. Thut. All but Bucholz and Bode were members of the Executive Board of the John Dewey Society in 1947.

The first appearance of the "By Way of Comment" section was in the November, 1946 issue of the journal. The section was identified as "Conducted by I. M. Thut" of the University of Connecticut. The section of the November, 1946 issue ran fifteen pages and opened with the following paragraph in an extended "Statement of Purpose":

> "By Way of Comment" is a new avenue for discussion that appears for the first time in this issue of *Educational Administration and Supervision*. It is projected by a small group of individuals who seek to call attention to the distinctive character of American education. It appears at this time because there is grave danger that teachers and others who are influential in shaping the future may lose their sense of direction amid the conflicting pressures stirred up by World War II, the disintegration of older patterns of social and moral values, and the ominous presence of a new monster—the atom bomb. (p. 462)

The statement closed with an open invitation to communicate with Thut or with the journal's editors concerning the "By Way of Comment" section. The members of the "small group" responsible for "By Way of Comment" were not identified as such, although the name of each contributor appeared below each of the items in the section. Over the period during which "By Way of Comment" appeared, many of the items were by members of the John Dewey Society, although the Society's sponsorship was never acknowledged. During 1947 and 1948, the "By Way of Comment" section included items by such figures as Ernest O. Melby, Ernest E. Bayles, John S. Brubacher, Prudence Bostwick, Harl R. Douglass, Everett J. Kircher, V. T. Thayer, Robert H. Beck, and Harold G. Shane. The items were timely, far-ranging, and lively—bearing such captions as "Education for Racial Harmony," "Democracy and Human Freedom," "A Truce Among Educators," "General Education and College Preparation," "On the Definition of Terms: Democracy," and "Education in the Atomic Age." The items also elicited some lively interactions, such as a response by Ernest Bayles of the University of Kansas to an item by M. H. Hedges, Director of Research of the International Brotherhood of Electrical Workers, which had stated that "Education is a process to enable the individual to adapt himself to his environment" (1947, p. 477). Taking sharp issue with the notion of adaptation, Bayles wrote:

> ... students should be trained in the progressive and continuous reconstruction of outlooks; independent reconstructions; that they be taught how to think. Instead of handing out ready-made conclusions, we should teach reflectively.
>   . . . education should strive to promote reflective studies which represent ideas in conflict, leading toward enhanced and more harmonic outlooks on life and heightened competence in the independent reconstruction of such outlooks. . . . Education should, in a very real sense, become preparation for politics. Schools cannot build a new social order, but they can do much toward assisting future citizens to become highly able participants in such building. (1948, p. 114)

For the most part, the "By Way of Comment" section reflected the experimentalist philosophy in addressing contemporary issues. The issue of the role of the school as a prime agency for social reconstruction was addressed in various publications of the Society over the years, but the main current was in the direction of the experimentalist perspective.

The last "By Way of Comment" section appeared in the December, 1949 issue of *Educational Administration and Supervision*—the last issue of an influential journal that had been published continuously for more than a third of a century. The more specialized journals of the professional associations in educational administration, teacher education, supervision, and curriculum development were making it increasingly difficult to continue the publication of independent journals such as *Educational Administration and Supervision*.

SPECIAL WRITING GRANTS

During the years following World War II, the minutes of the Executive Board meetings reveal extensive plans and discussions relating to the yearbook series and to the development of an expanded publications program. The minutes of the meetings on November 10–11, 1947 report that the Society had advanced five hundred dollars to Joseph Ratner for a biography of John Dewey, which was under contract with Oxford University Press. Since no yearbook was planned for 1948, it was agreed that explorations would be made to issue the Dewey biography in place of the yearbook. However, this never came about.

The minutes also report that several letters from John Dewey had urged the Society to provide some financial assistance for a writing project by Elsie Ripley Clapp. Elsie

Clapp had been an assistant to Dewey at Teachers College. Kilpatrick stated that John Dewey had agreed to write the introduction to the book. It was also noted that Miss Clapp had agreed to publish her book under the auspices of the Society in return for a writing grant. The Board decided to provide Miss Clapp with a writing grant of $600 on the condition that the Society would share in the royalties. Miss Clapp's book, *The Use of Resources in Education,* was published four years later (1952) by Harper & Row. The following statement appears at the top of the title page: "A Publication of the John Dewey Society." Although the book by Elsie Clapp is widely cited to this day in works on the history of education, the fact that the book was sponsored by the John Dewey Society is all but forgotten.

Elsie Clapp's book is a detailed and vivid account of the work done in a rural school in Jefferson County, Kentucky and in Arthurdale, West Virginia with the objective of developing people's resources in and through education by making the school integral to the functioning life of the community. Her account derives from her work as principal of the school in Jefferson County and later as director of the school and community activities in Arthurdale. The conditions of rural poverty in these communities during the Great Depression and the toll on children are movingly described by Elsie Clapp:

> The children in Nursery School in September looked like no little children we had ever known. Aged and wizened, wan and lifeless, they all showed the sufferings they had undergone. Most of them had either impetigo or scabies. Slowly, however, the daily care, good food, rest and fresh air, cod-liver oil and tomato juice, and the wise handling of apathies and emotional upsets took effect and the children began to grow younger, more

lively and less strained. Gradually, very gradually, the scabies and impetigo yielded to treatment, although it was spring before they were finally eradicated.

In the Big School, the children of different ages were variously affected by the hunger and misery they had undergone. . . . The children most injured were those between ten and fifteen whose development had been retarded by privation during their growing years and whose emotional stability was more or less shattered by their families' anxieties and distress, which they were old enough to share. The least difficulty brought anger and tears, and it was some time before their inner turmoil subsided. (p. 21)

The book opens with a selection, "In Appreciation," which states, "This book is, above all else, a tribute to John Dewey."

JOHN DEWEY'S LAST PUBLISHED STATEMENT

The Introduction, written by John Dewey, begins with the statement that Dewey considered it an honor, as well as an embarrassment to have been invited by the John Dewey Society to write the Introduction. In the Introduction, Dewey refrains from restating the basic ideas undergirding the work as described by Elsie Clapp, but provides the reader with an extensive statement about the whole movement of progressive education, "of which the work here described and interpreted is a part." After noting that during recent years, "organized attacks on the achievements of progressive education have become more extensive and virulent than ever before" in an effort "to turn the clock back in education," Dewey points out how the progressive education movement was part of the wider social movement for the improvement of the human condition. He then goes on to review some of the significant successes of progressive education, but also acknowledges the lack of progress in many quarters. "There is a great deal of talk about education being a cooperative enterprise in which teachers and students participate democratically," "but there is far more talk about it than doing it," writes Dewey. He then states, "It should be a commonplace, but unfortunately it is not, that no education—or anything else for that matter—is progressive unless it is making progress."

The Introduction to the book by Elsie Ripley Clapp for the John Dewey Society was Dewey's last published statement. He died on June 1, 1952 at the age of ninety-three.

The Board minutes of February 23, 1948 report that other writing grants had been made by the Society for book-length projects by individual authors on subjects of interest to the Society. However, the nature of these books and the identification of the authors were not revealed.

EDUCATION AND ACTION FOR DEMOCRACY

As noted earlier, the minutes of the Executive Board meetings in April, 1947 had expressed concern over "the low state to which faith in the democratic process has fallen." One of the measures taken by the Society was the creation of a Commission on Communication of Democracy through Education, chaired by William Van Til. At the meeting of the Board on November 10–11, 1947, Van Til stated that he was having some difficulty in defining the function of the Commission. Nevertheless, he proceeded to outline rather explicitly his conception of the activities of the Commission in promoting democracy through education:

(1) Preparing pamphlets to simplify to a maximum the ideas in the concept of democratic education
(2) Finding people who can break into the journalistic field, in behalf of the democratic point of view
(3) Occasionally stepping into local trouble spots to strengthen the hands of the local individuals or agencies who are fighting for a more democratic school

Considering that the Board had clearly established that the Society should not think of itself as an action group, it is surprising that the minutes of the Board meeting of November 10–11, 1947 do not reveal any debate concerning the Society's proposed role of "occasionally stepping into local trouble spots." Moreover, the minutes reveal that the Board was willing to "experiment" behind the scenes in a situation in Springfield, Missouri involving conservative attacks on the public schools and violations of academic freedom. As reported in the minutes:

> He (Van Til) did report that a particular situation in Springfield, Missouri led him to believe the commission might function in "spot" attacks on local schools. He requested the board to authorize him to experiment with the Springfield situation. On his motion, it was noted that the board appropriate up to $30 for the use of the commission in the Springfield situation. It was stipulated, however, that the work should be reported as that of an individual rather than that of a Society. This precaution was urged in order that the local progressive forces might not be subject to the "kiss of death" should it be reported that an outside agency is entering the situation.

The Board minutes for the meeting the following year (November 22–23, 1948) in New York City state that:

> Mr. Van Til, reporting for the Commission for the Communication of Democracy through Education,

brought before the Board data showing that the commission apparently had exerted a helpful influence in the Springfield, Missouri situation. This was made the basis for the suggestion that the Society in general and the commission in particular give some thought to how we can be helpful in other critical situations. He also reported on a study of the educational attitudes of and coverage given to educational matters by lay journals. It was felt that a study of this kind, properly publicized, might exert a good influence on such lay journals.

No elaboration was made concerning the actual actions of the Commission in the Springfield, Missouri situation, but apparently the Board's allocation of "up to $30" for the use of the Commission in the Springfield, Missouri situation was money well spent, if it was spent at all.

In 1947, the report of a joint committee of the Dewey Society and the Association for Supervision and Curriculum Development was submitted to the Society's Board at its meeting of November 10–11. The plan, "A Project for the Improvement of Education and the Welfare of the Young through Community Action," had been prepared by Gertrude Hankamp and Paul Misner of ASCD, and I. N. Thut and William Van Til of the Dewey Society. The plan called for the organization of local community action groups into a national federation to promote the public support of democratic public education. Although the Board authorized the continued explorations of the project with ASCD, the minutes state that "the Board was reluctant to consider the project one of sufficient distinctive character to warrant enthusiastic support." The project was later dropped for lack of financial support and organized interest.

XII

SEEKING TO SAVE
PROGRESSIVE EDUCATION

The report on *Progressive Education* revealed a losing
battle.
> —Board minutes, March 16, 1957

Within two years following the publication of the 1953
yearbook of the John Dewey Society, *Educational Freedom
in an Age of Anxiety,* edited by H. Gordon Hullfish, who
was then serving as President of the Progressive Education Association (PEA), Hullfish was forced to announce
the end of the PEA in the face of declining membership, at
a time of heightened assaults against progressive education and progressive social ideas. (The PEA membership
had reached a peak of 10,440 in 1938.) The Progressive
Education Association, which had changed its name to the
American Education Fellowship in 1944, had readopted
its original name in 1953, just two years before its demise.
The John Dewey Society sought to save the PEA's magazine, *Progressive Education,* and continued its publication
through 1957. *Progressive Education* dated back to 1924.
"Richly illustrated and extraordinarily attractive in format,
it presented news of progressive experiments in the United
States and in Western Europe," wrote Cremin in describing
the early years of the magazine (1961, p. 147).

The issues of *Progressive Education* from January 1956 to July 1957 were published by the John Dewey Society under the editorship of Lawrence E. Metcalf of the University of Illinois. Although the journal had lost much of the vivid and exciting quality of its early years, the period marking the final stage of its existence, when it was sponsored by the John Dewey Society, found penetrating articles in its pages on timely educational problems. For example, the March 1956 issue featured articles on school desegregation, including one by Kilpatrick titled "Modern Educational Theory and the Inherent Inequality of Segregation." The issues of January and May of 1956 included articles on critical thinking, with the latter issue of the journal also containing an article on academic freedom by H. Gordon Hullfish. The September 1956 issue featured the theme of "Religion and Education." The puzzling lead article in the November 1956 issue of *Progressive Education* by Fred N. Kerlinger of New York University, "The Origin of the Doctrine of Permissiveness in American Education," contended that permissiveness was based upon the thinking and work of Dewey as well as Freud. Identifying Dewey's theory of interest as "perhaps the most influential in giving educators a rationale for their doctrine of permissiveness," Kerlinger claimed that "Dewey also said that children 'learn by doing'" (p. 163). Oddly, no rejoinder appeared in that or any subsequent issue of *Progressive Education* to point out that Dewey never held that children "learn by doing," and that he had repeatedly attacked the emptiness of activity without guided intelligence and the emptiness of sheer permissiveness. (See, for example, John Dewey, *The Child and the Curriculum*, 1902.)

Be that as it may, the March 1957 issue of *Progressive Education* honored William H. Kilpatrick on his eighty-fifth birthday (November 16, 1956) with articles by John L. Childs, George Axtelle, R. Bruce Raup, and Roma Gans. The issue of May 1957 featured articles on democratic education by Ernest E. Bayles and H. Gordon Hullfish.

The last issue of *Progressive Education* appeared in July 1957, and was devoted to an assessment of the National Education Association on its 100th anniversary. The articles were critical of the NEA for its lack of militancy, administrator dominance of the organization, and its failure generally to find fault with American public education (acknowledging that "there is a critic of American public education behind every bush," p. 105). Nevertheless, a provocative article by William H. Brickman of New York University paid tribute to "the profound contribution of the NEA to the history of education in the United States and to its pedagogical literature" (pp. 111–115). Brickman went on to note the work of the various NEA committees over its history, including the signal contributions of the Educational Policies Commission, and the recorded addresses in the NEA *Proceedings*—such as those by such figures as Henry Barnard, G. Stanley Hall, Francis W. Parker, Josiah Royce, and Booker T. Washington during the last quarter of the nineteenth century.

The fateful decision to terminate publication of *Progressive Education* was made at the meeting of the Executive Committee of the John Dewey Society held in St. Louis on March 16, 1957. Although Kilpatrick was to finish his last term as President that year, to be succeeded by H. Gordon Hullfish, Kilpatrick was not at the meeting. (Kilpatrick was ending his nineteenth consecutive one-year term as President.) The minutes of the meeting, written by Hullfish, reveal that the business at hand was mainly concerned with the publications of the Society. The first item on the agenda was the losing battle of the Society in keeping *Progressive Education* alive, as revealed by the following extract from the minutes:

> The report on *Progressive Education* revealed a losing battle. An extensive effort was made this past year to secure advertising for the magazine. No success was had. More than forty publishers of textbooks and educational materials were contacted and but one advertisement was secured (and this through a personal letter of the President to his publisher.) One unsolicited advertisement was received. The advertisement carried somewhat regularly from The Interstate Printers is in accordance with arrangements made with them to reduce the debt remaining at the time of the dissolution of the Progressive Education Association. At the present time *Progressive Education* is losing approximately $200 an issue and with a further rise in printing costs on January 1st, the figure will approach $300. This, despite the series of notices developed and used in dealing with expirations; and, further, what the office views as a steadily improved magazine. (March 16, 1957)

A note to the minutes stated that since that meeting, Hullfish had asked President Harold Taylor of Sarah Lawrence College and President Hollis Caswell of Teachers College if either of their institutions would be able to continue the publication of *Progressive Education*, but the response was negative. The Society ended publication of *Progressive Education* with the issue of July, 1957.

Except for a brief item by H. Gordon Hullfish captioned "Hail and Farewell!," appearing near the final page of the journal, none of the articles in that issue gave any indication that the end had come at the midpoint of its thirty-fourth year of continuous publication. Most of the announcement by Hullfish was devoted to explaining that subscribers would receive refunds upon request or would be given the option of having their subscriptions transferred to *The Education Digest*. It was also stated that certain subscribers would be asked to waive their refund by making it a contribution to the John Dewey Society. The announcement explained that the continuing deficit of *Progressive Education* had "placed a drain on the resources of The John Dewey Society which it can no longer stand."

The tribute en toto given to *Progressive Education* in the announcement by Hullfish was as follows:

> With this issue of *Progressive Education* a faithful servant departs from the American educational scene. It does so with regret. It departs, however, with a realization that it has been a responsible participant in some of the more constructive thinking that has changed the face of American education for the better. . . .
>
> Readers of *Progressive Education* will not be surprised to discover that the magazine ended as it started, as a constructive critic of educational thought and practice. (p. 119)

The inside cover of the last issue of *Progressive Education* carried a list of the officers and members of the Executive Board and commissions of the John Dewey Society along with a statement on the Society's purposes and activities.

HAIL AND FAREWELL!

With this issue of PROGRESSIVE EDU-CATION a faithful servant departs from the American educational scene. It does so with regret. It departs, however, with a realization that it has been a responsible participant in some of the more constructive thinking that has changed the face of American education for the better.

Progressive Education closes shop with this, the July, 1957, issue. All who have had the responsibility for terminating publication at this point have reached this decision reluctantly. Yet they have had no live alternative. A continuing deficit, and a growing one with each issue, has placed a drain on the resources of The John Dewey Society which it can no longer stand. Had not sentiment prevailed up to this moment *Progressive Education* would have been discontinued months ago.

It is not easy to stop publication of a magazine which has gone to the midpoint in its 34th volume. Quite apart from sentiment, obligations exist to all who have subscribed, some throughout all of the years of its publication. The John Dewey Society will assume its obligations on this score, returning to each subscriber who asks for it the cash value of the unexpired subscription. This it will do at the earliest possible moment. It is asking certain subscribers, however, to make a contribution to the Society, by waiving this claim to a subscription refund. If this claim is waived generally, the Society, in turn, will be better able to continue its contribution to educational thought through its yearbooks and annual meetings. Fortunately, in no case is the sum involved large for the individual, though the total for the Society is considerable.

Some subscribers will not be asked to waive a subscription refund claim. Their subscriptions are to be completed by *The Education Digest*. The Editor of this publication has agreed to take over the subscription responsibility of *Progressive Education* in those instances where its readers are not currently subscribing to *The Education Digest*. As a matter of interest, this number is just under 50 per cent of the total subscribers to *Progressive Education*.

Readers of *Progressive Education* will not be surprised to discover that the magazine ends as it started, as a constructive critic of educational thought and practice. Its final issue is devoted to an analysis of the meaning for American life and education of the centennial which the National Education Association is now celebrating.

> H. Gordon Hullfish
> Executive Secretary-Treasurer
> The John Dewey Society

Columbus, Ohio
June, 1957

XIII

THE YEARBOOKS

No important problems were dodged; no conditions
which could be documented were ignored.
—Harold O. Rugg

Over a period spanning a quarter of a century, the John
Dewey Society issued sixteen yearbooks. Four of the
first ten yearbooks carried the term "democracy" in their
titles—a term that became noticeably less popular in the
lexicon of American public education since the late 1950s.
And virtually all of the yearbooks were focused on the pervasive issues of American democracy. (Even a casual count
of entries under the subject of "democracy" in the *Education Index* will reveal the sharp decline in the use of the
term from the time of the Cold War and space race extend-
ing into the 1980s.)

The first yearbook of the John Dewey Society was
issued in 1937, the last in 1962. In *The Transformation of the
School*, Lawrence Cremin makes note of the significance
of the yearbooks and lists several of them (p. 229). In *The
Foundations of American Education*, Harold Rugg wrote of
the yearbooks: "all are fresh and direct studies of education
in the actual framework of our changing American life. No
important problems were dodged; no conditions which
could be documented were ignored" (p. 579).

The first yearbook (1937), *The Teacher and Society*, was edited by William Kilpatrick with contributions from John Dewey, George H. Hartmann, Ernest O. Melby, Jesse Newlon, George D. Stoddard, Hilda Taba, Goodwin Watson, and Laura Zirbes. All but Melby, Taba, and Zirbes were founding members of the Society. Melby was Dean of the School of Education at Northwestern University.

In the Foreword of the first yearbook, Kilpatrick wrote, "In plan and procedure it follows generally the model of the National Society for the Study of Education." However, the Dewey Society yearbooks immediately took on a powerful character or identity of their own. This identity was well established in the first yearbook, which focused on the role of the teacher in a democratic society. Hard-hitting chapters addressed the problems faced by teachers—from their low economic status, to the poor conditions under which they must work; from their inadequate preparation, to barriers to their freedom to teach.

A chapter by George Hartmann in the first yearbook reported on the findings from a national survey in 1936 of the social attitudes of American secondary school teachers, sponsored by the Dewey Society. Usable returns were secured from 3,700 teachers in forty-three states (state education authorities in five states refused to cooperate with the survey). The random survey elicited a response of forty percent. The attitude survey was coupled with a Public Problems Information Test to assay teachers' knowledge of current affairs. It was found that the more knowledgeable teachers were those who were liberal or progressive in their outlook on social issues. All of the respondents agreed with the item, "Education should develop among its beneficiaries a disposition to participate ethically and intelligently in the solution of social problems." Only sixteen percent of the teachers disagreed with the statement, "It is pedagogically unprofitable to discuss serious social problems with adolescent youngsters." And only thirteen percent agreed that, "Teachers have a moral obligation to remain rigorously neutral on all debatable issues, both in class and out." Eighty seven percent disagreed that "There is no such thing as a class struggle in American life today." In his concluding comments, Hartmann pointed out that "American teachers are overwhelmingly committed to a policy of unceasing improvement of the quality of life's experiences for all Americans." But then he asked whether the nation's teachers are prepared to assist in this effort. "To meet this challenge may be the foremost professional task of our generation" (Hartmann in Kilpatrick (ed.), 1937, pp. 174–230).

The theme of academic freedom for the teacher, the pupil, and the curriculum in the schools of a free society was carried through successive yearbooks—from the 1938 yearbook, *Education and Democracy*, edited by Harold B. Alberty and Boyd H. Bode, and the 1939 yearbook, *Democracy and the Curriculum*, edited by Harold Rugg, to the 1953 yearbook, *Educational Freedom in an Age of Anxiety*, edited by H. Gordon Hullfish.

The minutes of the Executive Board meeting of February 23, 1941 report that the first four yearbooks of the Society were selling well and that a new contract with Harper & Brothers had been signed. Of the first four yearbooks, the third yearbook (1939), *Democracy and the Curriculum*, edited by Harold Rugg, was the best seller, with 5,481 copies sold in its first year of publication. The 1939 yearbook included chapters by Harold Rugg, Hollis L. Caswell, George S. Counts, and William H. Kilpatrick of Teachers College, George E. Axtelle of Northwestern University,

Paul R. Hanna of Stanford University, Pickens E. Harris of the University of Pittsburgh, Beryl Parker of New York University, and Caroline B. Zachry of the Progressive Education Association.

"THE AMERICAN PROBLEM"

The subtitle of the 1939 yearbook, *The Life and Program of the School*, reveals the experimentalist conception of the curriculum as far more than the formal subjects of study. Moreover, the 1939 yearbook addressed the curriculum problem in the light of the concept, "The American Problem" of the Great Depression. Although most of the contributors viewed the problems addressed in the 1939 yearbook through the experimentalist lens, Rugg's chapters reflect elements of the reconstructionist position born of the great social and economic dislocations of the Great Depression and the rising threat of totalitarian regimes on the global scene.

In the Foreword, Rugg identifies the factors associated with the need to attack "The American Problem"— the domination of vested interests over the wider public interest, the vulnerability of the people to propaganda, the great lag between economic production and distribution, and "the failure of mass education really to practice the democratic method and to build a program of study and discussion of the conditions and problems of life as it is actually lived today." Such factors are juxtaposed against the "national conviction that the free play of intelligence among the people should determine social policies," and the "commitment of the people to that unique form of life called 'American' democracy—the crux of which is freedom of utterance and maximum development for each individual . . . a society devoid as possible of social 'classes'" (pp. vi–vii).

In the opening chapter, Rugg proposes that, with the end of the geographic frontier, the time was long overdue to advance on the educational frontier. "To gather together the makings of the Great Society that are at hand, and to organize them into a growing national concern that will produce economic abundance, democratic behavior, and creative expression—that is the problem of our times," writes Rugg, to which he adds: "But—this must be done by the democratic method—by 'the American way.'"

Much of the material in the 1939 yearbook is remarkably germane to the curriculum problems of contemporary times. Rugg points out how universal literacy education may have been necessary in the first stage of industrial society, but it was only "a formal mechanism lacking dynamic functioning power" (p. 13). The curriculum of the schools must go far beyond this narrow function if education is to have dynamic functioning power for a democratic society (pp. 7–8, 13). (Ironically, the literacy function came to be revivified during the 1980s and again today, with high-stakes testing, capping a long period of educational retrenchment through "back-to-basics.")

A penetrating chapter by Pickens E. Harris shows how the schools tend to reflect the wider culture without coping with it, and how the curriculum is compartmentalized, isolated, and lacking a coherent design—with emphasis on technical mechanisms rather than interpretative processes. "Daily practice consists of numerous efficiency routines and an exaggerated administrative consciousness" (p. 170). Harris goes on to address the failure of the curriculum to "build any driving social enthusiasm" in our youth. "The typical curriculum, with its static logic and artificially shredded offerings, reflects no unifying ethical passion," writes Harris, and, "The excessive devotion to adult standards of mastery and coverage sickens the spontaneity of the young and degrades their potential eagerness to identify themselves with worthy social causes" (p. 181). Other chapters in the 1939 yearbook address the approaches to curriculum design and present descriptions of promising programs throughout the United States. Again, one may very easily change the date of the material to "2015" and find it valid and useful, as well as disturbingly penetrating.

The ninth yearbook, *Intercultural Attitudes in the Making*, issued in 1947 and edited by William Kilpatrick and William Van Til, examined the pernicious and persistent problem of discrimination against minorities and the role of the school in promoting intercultural education. Ironically, toward the close of the twentieth century, the focus shifted from intercultural education to multicultural education. Arthur Schlesinger, Jr. raised the issue questioning whether this shift signaled a "disuniting" of America (1998), but the multicultural emphasis persisted amidst great gains in civil rights. Nevertheless, the very concept of *intercultural* education, advanced by the John Dewey Society following the end of World War II, proved to be timely and prophetic.

AGE OF ANXIETY

The 1953 yearbook was issued at the height of McCarthyism. As editor of the yearbook, H. Gordon Hullfish of Ohio State University criticized the special loyalty oaths required of teachers, the banning of books, and the restrictions against the voicing of ideas in school and college—actions that only serve to undermine the very foundations of the society that they are allegedly designed to protect.

In 1953 most of the states required a loyalty oath as a condition of employment of teachers in the public schools or professors in public institutions of higher education. President Truman's Loyalty Oath of 1947 required a loyalty investigation of every prospective federal employee, and one of the standards for refusal of employment was to be "membership in, affiliation with or *sympathetic association* with any . . . organization, association, movement, *group or combination* of persons, designated by the Attorney General as . . . *subversive* . . ." (*Federal Register*, Vol. 12, p. 1935, ital. in the original). Truman's Loyalty Oath was followed by a climate in which academic freedom was being severely threatened. "Guilt by association" provided a field day for the ultra-right in attacking individuals and groups espousing progressive ideas. The term *progressive* was used disparagingly if not suspiciously. In an article in 1951 marking William Kilpatrick's eightieth birthday, *The New York Times* noted that Kilpatrick preferred the term "modern education" to progressive education (November 17, 1951, p. 19).

To be progressive means to be making progress. "No idea has been more important," wrote Robert Nisbet, "than the idea of progress in Western civilization" (1980, p. ix). But he observed that the idea was falling in the twentieth century and warned that, "If the idea of progress does die in the West, so will a great deal that we have long cherished in this civilization" (p. 4).

Under the climate of the times, the 1953 yearbook of the John Dewey Society was aptly titled *Educational Freedom in an Age of Anxiety*. In the yearbook, H. Gordon Hullfish drew upon Dewey in pointing to the fallacy and delusion of employing authoritarian means in the name of democratic ends (pp. 214–215). John L. Childs offered an extended statement on the mission and contributions of the John Dewey Society from the time of its inception. His statement read in part as follows:

> One of the primary contributions of John Dewey has been the development of an educational theory and practice which is an integrated expression of both the values of democracy and the method of experimental inquiry. The Society which bears his name was founded by a group of educators who wanted to give public recognition to their acceptance of the main elements in this democratic and scientific orientation. These educators had no thought of turning the educational views of Dewey into a new orthodoxy; on the contrary, they were concerned to use them as a method of intellectual and moral approach to the novel situations they knew they were sure to encounter in a world in which "change and uncertainty are ultimate traits," . . .
>
> Most of the founders of the John Dewey Society perceived that we were entering upon a period of cultural transformation and transition. They realized that science and technology were drastically altering the conditions of human living. Earlier than many groups, these educators recognized that basic adjustments would have to be made in historic American attitudes and institutionalized arrangements if efficient democratic use was to be made of our rapidly expanding powers of agricultural and industrial production. They realized that new conceptions of human rights and responsibilities were required. . . .

The founders of the John Dewey Society also had faith that the American people would succeed in working out these necessary adjustments in their modes of thinking as well as in their ways of living. They were united in the purpose to

make organized education play its part on the social frontier of American life where these new patterns of human
relationship, of human rights and responsibilities, of economic and governmental forms were in process of development and formulation (pp. 186–187).

XIV

THE LAST OF THE YEARBOOKS AND THE BEGINNING OF THE LECTURE SERIES

The schools are in the unfortunate position of having
a bear by the tail.
—Boyd H. Bode, Second Yearbook,
John Dewey Society, 1938

The minutes of the Executive Board meeting of March 16, 1957 also included a report by Archibald Anderson for the Society's Commission on Yearbooks, in which it was recommended that the yearbooks be terminated with the publication of the manuscripts then at hand. It was stated that the yearbook pattern "had played out," and it was agreed that the publications program of the Society should be continued in some other form. The motion to terminate the Yearbook Series was passed unanimously. The last yearbook, *Negro Education in America*, was published in 1962.

In retrospect, one might be puzzled as to how the John Dewey Society came to sponsor such contrasting publications as *The Social Frontier* and *Progressive Education*. Although *The Social Frontier* was focused more directly and polemically on ideological issues concerning the role of public education in wider social reform, whereas *Progressive Education* was devoted principally to progressive reforms in educational practice with some consideration of social implications of such reforms, both publications were progressive in character and commitment. Moreover, several of the founding members of the John Dewey Society had contributed significantly to both publications. And, as noted earlier, although *The Social Frontier* and the John Dewey Society were not of the same progeny, the original editors and many of the initial Board of Directors of *The Social Frontier* were also among the sixty-seven founding members of the John Dewey Society.

Looking back, it seems remarkable that such a small organization as the John Dewey Society, with such very limited resources, should take on the task of attempting to save these two magazines under the most formidable conditions. Despite the eventual demise of *The Social Frontier* and *Progressive Education,* the role of the John Dewey Society in seeking to save these two unique magazines, which figures so visibly in such an important chapter of American education and society, is testimony to a courageous and unparalleled effort. The story of this effort has been largely unrecognized.

In retrospect, it is difficult to conceive that the yearbooks "had played out"—for they were vitally directed at the issues of the time and the contributors were national figures in education. No other publications of any kind could possibly fill the vacuum created by the termination of the Yearbook Series. Were the yearbooks terminated in view of financial constraints? This appears not to be the case, for the minutes of the Executive Board meeting five years later (February 15, 1962), chaired by H. Gordon Hullfish, indicated that the larger than usual balance in the Society's treasury was partly a result of the royalties from the yearbooks. It was also noted in the minutes that, "unless the Society publishes an occasional yearbook of general interest, it cannot look forward to as much income as it has had."

Perhaps the decision of the Executive Board on March 16, 1957 to terminate the Yearbook Series was a reflection of the tone of pessimism that surrounded the impending termination of the Society's sponsorship of *Progressive Education*. Yet at the meeting of March 16, 1957, the decision was made "in consideration of the publications program" to establish an annual John Dewey Lecture to be presented at the mid-winter meetings in Chicago of the American Association of Colleges for Teacher Education and to be published by the Society.

From 1961 to the present, the John Dewey Lecture has been published in book form. Although many of the published lectures were well received, the published Lecture Series never attained the recognition given the yearbooks. (After more than a quarter of a century of presenting the Dewey Lecture at the AACTE meetings in Chicago, the Lecture was moved in 1987 to the locale of the Annual Meeting of the American Educational Research Association.)

The decision of the Board at its 1957 meeting to establish the John Dewey Lecture bears significance in relation to the already established practice at that time of having three or so educators present lectures, under the auspices of the Society, on the eve of the Annual Meeting of the Association for Supervision and Curriculum Development. In 1949, William Van Til, who was to serve as President of the Society from 1964 to 1965, had initiated this session of lectures in conjunction with the ASCD meeting beginning in 1950. The Society had previously followed the practice of sponsoring one or more lectures on the eve of annual meetings of various national organizations, including the American Association of School Administrators. It will be recalled that the meetings of the Society at the annual convention of AASA had proved to be too controversial for the school administrators, so that the Society's request for space at the 1948 AASA convention in Atlantic City was ignored. As a result, the Society was to hold its annual meeting independently in Atlantic City for several years until it was to find a welcome home in Chicago at the site of the annual meetings of the American Association of Colleges for Teacher Education. The first John Dewey Lecture was delivered at the 1958 meeting of AACTE, with Ordway Tead speaking on "The Climate of Learning." Although some of the lectures over the years were to focus on Dewey or to reflect Dewey's experimentalist philosophy (such as Oscar Handlin, "John Dewey's Challenge to Education," 1959, and Gardner Murphy, "Freeing Intelligence through Teaching," 1960, most were highly diverse in outlook. In this respect, the John Dewey Lecture series contrasts sharply with the Yearbook series (1937–1962) which explicated a powerful experimentalist perspective. (The John Dewey Lecture was published in expanded book form almost every year from 1958 to 2006. The published lectures are listed in the Appendix.)

In contrast to the annual John Dewey Lecture, which has tended to be theoretical in nature, the John Dewey Memorial Lecture held annually with ASCD since 1950 has featured leading educators addressing a wide range of timely and powerful topics and issues—such as academic freedom, general education, education for a world society, school desegregation, Soviet education, poverty in America, teacher education, the federal role in education, the teacher's responsibilities in curriculum development, and so on. The John Dewey Memorial ASCD Lecture is not to be confused with the Society's John Dewey Lecture, which was presented at the annual meeting in Chicago of the American Association of Colleges for Teacher Education during the period from 1958 to 1986, and, since 1987, at the location of the annual meeting of the American Educational Research Association. Known as The John Dewey Memorial Lecture, the ASCD series was sponsored with the John Dewey Society and was presented at the ASCD Annual Convention. The ASCD series featured such educators as Ernest O. Melby (1950), George S. Counts (1951), Willard Goslin (1952), B. O. Smith and H. Gordon Hullfish (1953), J. Paul Leonard and Malkolm MacLean (1954), R. Freeman Butts and William H. Kilpatrick (1956).

Goslin, who had been a member of the Executive Board of the John Dewey Society during the late 1940s, was the subject of a widely read and hotly debated book, *This Happened in Pasadena* (1951) by David Hulburd. Hulburd's book related how Willard Goslin, a highly respected educator, had been ousted from his position as Pasadena's school superintendent by a coalition opposed to progressive education and school taxes. The book related how a noted educator and an effective educational program had been brought down unfairly, and how the event could happen in other communities.

As noted above, among the other speakers at these ASCD sessions sponsored by the Dewey Society were Malcolm MacLean, Director of the notably experimental General College at the University of Minnesota, and J. Paul Leonard, who, as president of San Francisco State College, had initiated an experimental undergraduate curriculum in general education based upon the psychosocial development of young adults. A list of the speakers since 1950 is presented in the Appendix.

It will be recalled that Henry Harap, who had taken the first step leading to the founding of the John Dewey Society, also took the initiative in the founding of the Society for Curriculum Study, which later became the Association for Supervision and Curriculum Development.

Unfortunately, for some inexplicable reason, the John Dewey Society discontinued its co-sponsorship of the Memorial Lecture with ASCD in 2005—a series that dated back to 1950. However, ASCD continued the lecture series without co-sponsorship with the Dewey Society. Renewal of co-sponsorship would reconnect the Dewey Society with one of its last direct organizational links with school leaders. It should be added that, whereas the Dewey Society had selected the speakers for the ASCD Memorial Lecture from 1950 to 2005, the speakers since 2005 were leaders in the curriculum field and more directly connected with the interests of the ASCD members. The speaker for 2013 notably was Justice Sandra Day O'Connor, the first woman appointed to the U.S. Supreme Court. Justice O'Connor spoke on the need to restore and revitalize civics for democracy in the school curriculum.

In 2006, the John Dewey Society published the last John Dewey Lecture, although the Lecture continues to be delivered at the Society's Annual Meeting to this day. At one point, under the leadership of Jonas E. Soltis, president of the Society (1990-1991), the Dewey Lecture was presented at Teachers College, Columbia University, several weeks following delivery at the Society's Annual Meeting. This annual published lecture series had dated back to 1958. The early lectures were published by Harper, and the last by Teachers College Press. Failure of speakers to present publishable book-length manuscripts coupled with the declining readership had become a growing problem.

The last issue of the Society's publication, *Insights*, under the editorship of Jon G. Bradley, appeared in 2011. *Insights* had been launched in 1964 as a medium for addressing current concerns, issues, and opinions. Under Bradley's editorship, *Insights* had become an attractive journal physically, as well as an informed and popular medium for the Society's activities and concerns.

In 2002, under President Daniel Tanner, the Society established the Annual John Dewey Society Symposium with the purpose of examining critical issues concerning the public schools. The symposium has been a popular event on the Society's annual program.

In 2011 the Society's journal, *Education and Culture*, took on a new look under the editorship of A. G. Rud. However, the focus of *Education and Culture* was concentrated mainly on educational theory. That same year, Tanner raised the status of the Society's Committee on Social Issues to that of a Commission, with the charge to draft periodic position papers to be issued by the Society in response to the destructive attacks on the nation's public schools. However, no position papers were published for issuance by the Society.

In the words of the original Constitution of the John Dewey Society, adopted in 1935, "The purpose of the society is to foster scholarly and scientific investigation of problems pertaining to the place and function of education in social change, and to publish the results of such studies." From 1937 to 1962, the John Dewey Society published sixteen yearbooks that addressed the most significant educational topics and problems. The yearbooks were widely read and influential in advancing progressive educational policy and practice. From 1958 to 2006 the John Dewey Society published twenty-eight of its lectures, most of which were favorably regarded.

Recognizing the decline of its publications and research-action programs, in 2013 the Society dropped the terms "publish" and "investigation" from the stated purpose of the Society. Yet "scholarship" and "publication" must be recognized as inseparably two sides of the same coin. In looking back on the history of the John Dewey Society, our perspective demands a concluding view of the prospects for the future of the Society.

XV
PERSPECTIVES AND PROSPECTS

The current effort to turn back the clock on education
is a real cause for alarm.

—John Dewey

Throughout most of its history the Dewey Society clearly
connected scholarship with democratic social cause and
activism in supporting and defending the public schools
against unwarranted attack. The John Dewey Society was
in the vanguard in addressing the most pervasive problems and issues in public education: academic freedom,
educational opportunity, racial discrimination, curriculum
experimentation, poverty and learning, school desegregation and integration, professionalization of teaching,
the comprehensive secondary school, educational and
social equity, high-stakes testing, educational freedom and
democracy, the classroom and school as a cooperative learning community, intercultural education, global education,
and so on. Were all these concerns and beyond too much
of an agenda? The answer is: How can they be distilled,
culled, and separated? They are all part of the American
experience and, as such, illumine the idea of progress. By
its very meaning, progress is not an end, but a continuing
journey for improving conditions by solving real problems.

TO RECLAIM A LEGACY

The mission of a professional school—whether of education, medicine, architecture, engineering or law—is to prepare those who are to engage in the practice of the profession and to advance professional practice through relevant research. Professional schools in a university are necessarily mission-oriented, not discipline-oriented. Except for its professional schools, institutes and centers for applied research, the traditional university is discipline-centered. Disciplinary boundaries and jurisdictions are zealously established and jealously guarded department by department. To paraphrase John Dewey, purity of knowledge, like traditional feminine chastity, requires all kinds of safeguards to hedge it about (1939, p. 152).

Beginning in the 1960s, many of our colleagues in the field of social and philosophical foundations of education turned away from the mission of their professional school and joined the school blamers, with damaging effect to teacher education and the work of the teacher (Engler, 1973; Ravitch, 1987). As a consequence, they became less relevant to the mission of a school of education in a university, and their ranks underwent a sharp decline from which the field has not recovered. A recovery is possible only if the mission-oriented legacy of the field is recognized and acted upon. This is a monumental task of rediscovery and renewal, but rediscovery and renewal are fundamental to the very idea of progress.

In his last published words before his death, John Dewey left this message in the Introduction to Elsie Ripley Clapp's book, The Use of Resources in Education, sponsored by the John Dewey Society:

During the past few years, organized attacks on the achievements of progressive education have become more extensive and virulent than ever before. The current effort to turn the clock back in education is a real cause for alarm but not for surprise. The educational system is part of the common life and cannot escape suffering the consequences that flow from the conditions prevailing outside the school building. When repressive and reactionary forces are increasing in strength in all our other social institutions—economic, social and political—it would be folly to expect the school to get off free. (p. viii)

Dewey's statement could well have been written today, and perhaps serves as a warning to the John Dewey Society of the danger of losing its way, and retreating to the safe confines of speculative theory and isolated academic association, while neglecting its origins of connecting with the concrete problems of school and society, child and curriculum. For Dewey, philosophy of education can be a source of a science of education only if it connects with educational practice by providing working hypotheses of comprehensive application (1929, p. 54). But he goes on to caution that,

Concrete educational experience is the primary source of all inquiry and reflection because it sets the problems, and tests, modifies, confirms or refutes the conclusions of intellectual investigation. The philosophy of education neither originates nor settles ends. It occupies an intermediate and instrumental or regulative place. Ends virtually reached, consequences that actually accrue, are surveyed, and their values estimated in the light of a general scheme of values.

But if a philosophy starts to reason out its conclusions without definite and constant regard to the concrete experiences that define the problem for thought, it becomes speculative in a way that justifies contempt. (1929, p. 56)

The contemporary scene, marked by new and old assaults against the public schools, including the movement to split up the school system by means of charter schools, would appear to give cause for the John Dewey Society to reclaim its founding vision and mission. But this would require a new turning point for renewal in creating concrete connections with educational practice, with child and curriculum, school and society.

The question must be raised as to whether the time was ripe for the John Dewey Society to reclaim its legacy of scholarship, publication and activism in advancing the mission of the public schools in a democratic society. This would require a new turning point for the Society—a turning point that might also reclaim the diversity and size of the membership, along with its founding mission and tradition of attacking the most pervasive issues of school and society.

Born in the hard times of the Great Depression, the John Dewey Society had many turning points throughout its early history. The turning points were taken for the most part not as insuperable obstacles, nor as signals to shift with the dominant tide of the times, but in the spirit of Dewey in seeing them as crossroads to "a continual beginning afresh" (1916, p. 417).

Such a "continuing beginning afresh" is not merely a matter of change, innovation, restructuring or reform. It is a matter of renewal for growth and progress.

APPENDIX

FOUNDING MEMBERS OF THE JOHN DEWEY SOCIETY

Homer Anderson	Superintendent of Schools, Omaha, NE
W. D. Armentrout	Colorado State Teachers College
Fred H. Bair	Superintendent of Schools, Shaker Heights, OH
Frank E. Baker	Milwaukee State Teachers College
Willard Beatty	Superintendent of Schools, Bronxville, NY
William Biddle	Colgate University
William D. Boutwell	*School Life*
O. G. Brim	The Ohio State University
—Bristol	Oakland, California, Public Schools
E. deS. Brunner	Teachers College
Oscar Buros	Rutgers University
Henry Busch	Cleveland College
H. L. Caswell	George Peabody College
John Childs	Teachers College
Harold Clark	Teachers College
Donald P. Cottrell	Teachers College
George S. Counts	Teachers College
S. A. Courtis	Detroit, Michigan
C. L. Cushman	Denver, Colorado
P. W. L. Cox	New York University
Edgar Dale	The Ohio State University
Newton Edwards	University of Chicago
George Frasier	Colorado State Teachers College
Willard Givens	National Education Association
Kenneth Gould	Scholastic Magazine

131

Mordecai Grossman	*The Social Frontier*
Harold Hand	Stanford University
Paul R. Hanna	Teachers College
Henry Harap	Western Reserve University
J. K. Hart	Hudson, New York
George Hartmann	State College, Pennsylvania
L. Thomas Hopkins	Teachers College
H. Gordon Hullfish	Dalton School, New York City
E. W. Jacobsen	Superintendent of Schools, Oakland, CA
F. Ernest Johnson	Teachers College
Grayson Kefauver	Stanford University
W. H. Kilpatrick	Teachers College
Marvin Krueger	600 West End Avenue, New York City
Rudolph Lindquist	The Ohio State University
Forrest E. Long	New York University
A. Gordon Melvin	College of the City of New York
Clyde R. Miller	Teachers College
Theodore Newcomb	Bennington College
Jesse H. Newlon	Teachers College
Daniel Prescott	Rutgers University
R. Bruce Raup	Teachers College
Frederick Redefer	Progressive Education Association
Rollo G. Reynolds	Teachers College
Holland Roberts	Principal, Harrison High School, Harrison, NY
Maurice Robinson	*Scholastic Magazine*
Earle Rugg	Colorado State Teachers College
Harold Rugg	Teachers College
Edward Sanders	Colgate University
Laurence Sears	Ohio Wesleyan University
James M. Shields	Alexandria, VA
Robert Speer	New York University
Ralph B. Spence	Teachers College
George Stoddard	University of Iowa
J. W. Studebaker	U.S. Commissioner of Education
A. L. Threlkeld	Superintendent of Schools, Denver, CO
I. Keith Tyler	The Ohio State University
Ralph W. Tyler	The Ohio State University
Carleton Washburne	Superintendent of Schools, Winnetka, IL
John Washburne	Syracuse University, Syracuse, NY
Goodwin Watson	Teachers College
Norman Woelfel	The Social Frontier, 509 West 121st St., N.Y.C.
Harvey Zorbaugh	35 West Fourth Street, New York City

YEARBOOKS OF THE JOHN DEWEY SOCIETY

The sixteen yearbooks issued by the Society from 1937 to 1962, along with their editors, are listed in chronological order as follows:

    I. William H. Kilpatrick (ed.), *The Teacher and Society*. New York: D. Appleton-Century (1937).

    II. Harold B. Alberty and Boyd H. Bode (eds.), *Educational Freedom and Democracy*. New York: D. Appleton-Century (1938).

    III. Harold Rugg (ed.), *Democracy and the Curriculum*. New York: D. Appleton-Century (1939).

    IV. George E. Axtelle and William H. Wattenberg (eds.), *Teachers for Democracy*. New York: D. Appleton-Century (1940).

    V. Theodore Brameld (ed.), *Workers' Education in the United States*. New York: D. Appleton-Century (1941).

    VI. Ernest O. Melby (ed.), *Mobilizing Educational Resources*. New York: Harper & Brothers (1943).

    VII. John S. Brubacher (ed.), *The Public School and Spiritual Values*. New York: Harper & Brothers (1944).

    VIII. Hollis L. Caswell (ed.), *The American High School*. New York: Harper & Brothers (1946).

    IX. William H. Kilpatrick and William Van Til (eds.), *Intercultural Attitudes in the Making*. New York: Harper & Brothers (1947).

    X. Harold Benjamin (ed.), *Democracy in the Administration of Higher Education*. New York: Harper & Brothers (1950).

    XI. Christian O. Arndt and Samuel Everett (eds.), *Education for a World Society*. New York: Harper & Brothers (1951).

    XII. H. Gordon Hullfish (ed.), *Educational Freedom in an Age of Anxiety*. New York: Harper & Brothers (1953).

    XIII. Harold G. Shane (ed.), *The American Elementary School*. New York: Harper & Brothers (1953).

    XIV. Lindley J. Stiles (ed.), *The Teacher's Role in American Society*. New York: Harper & Brothers (1957).

    XV. Samuel Everett (ed.), *Programs for the Gifted*. New York: Harper & Brothers (1961).

    XVI. Virgil Clift et al. (eds.), *Negro Education in America*. New York: Harper & Brothers (1962).

THE JOHN DEWEY MEMORIAL ASCD LECTURES
(ASSOCIATION FOR SUPERVISION
AND CURRICULAR DEVELOPMENT)

TOPIC	SPEAKERS
1950 Why General Education in the Public Schools	Ernest O. Melby, Robert F. Gilchrist, William Van Til
1951 Education for a World Society	C. O. Arndt, George S. Counts, Samuel Everett
1952 Educational Freedom in an Age of Anxiety	William H. Burton, Willard Goslin
1953 What's Ahead for Progressive Education	Miles Cary, B. Othanel Smith, H. Gordon Hullfish
1954 Education for American Freedom	J. Paul Leonard, F. Torsten Lund, Malcolm MacLean
1955 Report on Integration and Segregation	Dan Dodson, George Mitchell, E. T. McSwain
1956 Religion and Education	R. Freeman Butts, George Reavis, Jerome Nathanson, F. Ernest Johnson, William Heard Kilpatrick
1957 The Intellectual Component of Modern Education	B. Othanel Smith, H. Gordon Hullfish, Archibald Anderson, Charles Wilson, Rev. R. J. Henle, Jennie Wahlert
1958 Rockets, Satellites, and Missiles: Their Meaning for American Education	Paul DeHart Hurd, Willard Spalding, Fred T. Wilhelms, Arno A. Bellack

1959

John Dewey: Exponent of Intellectual Discipline

B. Othanel Smith, Joe Park,
George E. Axtelle

1960

What Can We Really Learn From
Russian Education?

C. O. Arndt, George S. Counts,
William H. E. Johnson

1961

Who Is Being Heard in Education
Today?

Lindley G. Stiles, William Van Til

1962

The New Educational Technology and Organization—For
What?

James D. Finn, J. Lloyd Trump,
Robert Fleming

1963

How Can Our Profession
Achieve Better Salaries and
Conditions?

Walter A. Anderson, Joe Burnett,
Clarine Kline, Carl J. Megel

1964

The Education of American
Teachers: Agreements and
Issues

Merle Borrowman, George W.
Denemark, Florence Strate-
meyer, Harold Taylor

1965

Poverty in the United States:
What Can Education Do?

Virgil Clift, Raymond W. Mack,
Dan Schreiber

1966

Assessment of Federal Aid Programs: Are We Developing a
Third School System?

Margaret Gill, I. James Quillen,
Robert R. Smith

1967

Educational Technology and
Professional Practice

Francis A. Ianni, Richard I. Miller

1968

Troubles and Triumphs—And
What to Do Now?

Louis S. Levine, Frances R. Link,
Juliet Saunders

1969

Teacher Negotiations in the
Curriculum: The Curricular
Rights and Responsibilities of
Teachers

C. Taylor Whittier, Leslee Bishop

1970

Consequences of Confrontation

Alvin Loving, Robert R. Smith,
Staten Webster

1971

The Counterculture: What Can We Learn — Arthur G. Wirth, Joann Boydston, Sidney Simon

1972

Compulsory Education Under Fire — Harold G. Shane, Murel J. Clute, W. Richard Stephens

1973

Relative Influence of School and Society on Inequality — Robert Beck, John Mann, Duane Mattheis, James Phillips

1974

Unionism, Tenure, Academic Freedom — William L. Cunningham, R. J. Kibbee, Albert Shanker, John Vasconcellos

1975

Peoples Lib: How Women's Lib Is Affecting Male Lib? — James B. Macdonald, Helen James Wallace, Deborah P. Wolfe

1976

Education 1776–1976–2076: Where Are We Going? — Harold G. Shane, W. O. Stanley, Glenys Unruh

1977

Who Really Needs a College Degree—Your Child or Mine? — Nolan Estes, Simon O. Johnson, Karl Openshaw

1978

The Politics of Curriculum/Educational Decision Making: Who Should be Responsible for What? — Robert F. Alioto, Laurence Iannaccone, Francis R. Link

1979

Who Is Being Heard in Education Today? — Mario Fantini, Wilma Longstreet, William Van Til

1980

Propositions in Search of Curriculum: Dreams Yet Unfulfilled — William Alexander, Arthur W. Foshay

1981

Theory into Practice into Theory: A Realistic Cycle? — Louise Berman, Bruce Joyce, Louis Rubin

1982

How Should We Measure School Effectiveness? — Marilyn Hammond, William Ingram, Richard Schutz

1983

Problems and Concerns on the Eve of 1984: Censorship, Creationism, Computer Chips, and ???

Ron Brandt, Yvonne Ewell, Jack Frymier

1984

Recent Educational Reports vs. Back to the Basics: An Appraisal

Gerald Firth, Maxine Greene, Mary Anne Raywid, Daniel Tanner

1985

Reflections on Education: Where Have We Been and Where Are We Headed?

Ralph W. Tyler and Harry S. Broudy

1986

Educational Leadership: What Is Needed Today to Ensure Quality Instruction into the Next Century

Noreen Garman, Ben Harris, Robert Anderson

1987

An Era of Confusion in American Education: State Capitol vs. Independent School Districts as Centers for Reform

Laurel N. Tanner, Carolyn Highes, Dale Mann

1988

Conflicting Models of Instructional Supervision

Robert Anderson, Edith Grimsley, Gary Griffin

1989

Influence of Testing on the Curriculum

George F. Madaus, Susan Stodolsky

1990

Reforming the Schools: Is It Deja vu All Over Again?

Larry Cuban, Jane Stallings, Zalman Usiskin

1991

Putting the Pieces Together: Toward Comprehensive Program of School Reform

Luvern L. Curmingham, Henrietta Schwartz, Ralph W. Tyler

1992

Changing Demographics and the Curriculum: What Have We Learned and Where Are We Going?

Constance E. Clayton, A. Harry Passow, W. Robert Houston (Chair)

1993

Restructuring Schools: What Have We Learned?

Ann Lieberman, Joyce L. Epstein, William Georgiades

1994

National Education Standards: Threat or Promise?

Edgar G. Epps, Susan H. Fuhrman, Arthur E. Wise

1995

Helping Disadvantaged Students to Succeed: What Have We Learned?

Lucy Wong Fillmore, Bill Honig, Henry M. Levin

1996

Releasing Imagination in Educational Reform

Maxine Greene, Louise Berman, William Ayers

1997

A Sense of Vision and Purpose: Reflecting on John Dewey's 1897 Pedagogic Creed in 1997

Linda Darling-Hammond, Craig Kridel, Lucinda Lee Katz, Laurel Tanner

1998

Reclaiming the Heart and Soul of Teaching and Learning

James A. Beane, Carl D. Glickman, Gloria Ladson-Billings

1999

Schools We Need and Bridges to Them

Michele Foster, Paul S. Shaker, Decker F. Walker

2000

School and Nonschool Education in the New Millennium: The Mutual Influence

Alex Molnar, Wilma Longstreet, William Doll

2001

What Business Ought to Be Concerned About in American Education

David C. Berliner, Anna M. Austin, Dennis C. Buss

2002

Children, the Public Good, and the Myth of Accountability

Linda McNeil

2003

An Educational Rights Amendment

Joel Spring

2004

Meeting Literacy Standards Through Democratic Classrooms

Gay Su Pinnell, Eloise Hambright-Brown

2005	Ana Martinez Aleman, Robert
The Challenges of Latino Demographics to Educational Accountability in a Democracy	Starratt
2006	
Fighting for the Heart of Education: The New DEEL	Steven Jay Gross, Robert Starratt
2007	
Children's Social Consciousness and the Development of Social Responsibility	Sheldon Berman, Robert Starratt
2008	
Education for Democratic Citizenship: Leadership Challenges and Leadership Practices	Robert Starratt, Bruce Kramer
2009	
John Dewey's Vision of Progressive Laboratorial and Utopian Schools	Douglas Simpson
2010	
Promoting Cultural Understanding Through Music	Mary Goetze
2011	
The Flat World of Education	Linda Darling-Hammond
2012	
Revolutionizing Education	Alan Taylor
2013	
Not Your Grandmother's Civics: A Conversation with Justice Sandra Day O'Connor	Justice Sandra Day O'Connor
2014	
Repurposing American Schools	Carl Glickman

THE JOHN DEWEY LECTURES[1]

1958. Ordway Tead. *The Climate of Learning.* New York: Harper & Brothers.

1959. Oscar Handlin. *John Dewey's Challenge to Education.* New York: Harper & Brothers.

1960. Seymour E. Harris. *More Resources for Education.* New York: Harper & Brothers.

1961. Gardner Murphy. *Freeing Intelligence Through Teaching.* New York: Harper & Brothers.

1962. Loren Eiseley. *The Mind as Nature.* New York: Harper & Brothers.

1963. R. Freeman Butts. *American Education in International Development.* New York: Harper & Row.

1965. Houston Smith. *Condemned to Meaning.* New York: Harper & Row.

1966. Abraham Maslow. *The Psychology of Science.* New York: Harper & Row.

1967. Robert J. Schaefer. *The School as a Center of Inquiry.* New York: Harper & Row.

1968. Donald N. Michael. *The Unprepared Society.* New York: Basic Books.

1970. Bentley Glass. *The Timely and the Timeless.* New York: Basic Books.

1971. Robert Nisbet. *The Degradation of the Academic Dogma.* New York: Basic Books.

1973. Theodosius Dobzhansky. *Human Equality and Genetic Diversity.* New York: Basic Books.

1976. Lawrence A. Cremin. *Public Education.* New York: Basic Books.

1977. David Hawkins. *The Science and Ethics of Equality.* New York: Basic Books.

1981. Harry S. Broudy. *Truth and Credibility.* New York: Longman.

1982. Elliott W. Eisner. *Cognition and Curriculum.* New York: Longman.

1984. C. A. Bowers. *The Promise of Theory.* New York: Longman.

1984. Thomas F. Green. *The Formation of Conscience in an Age of Technology.* Syracuse, N.Y.: School of Education, Syracuse University.

1986. James Gouinlock. *Excellence in Public Discourse: John Stuart Mill, John Dewey, and Social Intelligence.* New York: Teachers College Press.

1988. Elsie Boulding. *Building a Global Culture: Education for an Independent World.* New York: Teachers College Press.

1988. Maxine Greene. *The Dialectic of Freedom*. New York: Teachers College Press.

1993. Nel Noddings. *Education for Intelligent Belief or Unbelief*. New York: Teachers College Press.

1996. Michael W. Apple. *Cultural Politics and Education*. New York: Teachers College Press.

1997. John I. Goodlad. *In Praise of Education*. New York: Teachers College Press.

2002. Philip W. Jackson. *John Dewey and the Philosopher's Task*. New York: Teachers College Press.

2004. Jane Roland Martin. *Cultural Miseducation in Search of a Democratic Solution*. New York: Teachers College Press.

2006. Jeannie Oakes and John Rogers. *Learning Power: Organizing for Education and Justice*. New York: Teachers College Press.

NOTES

1. Although the earliest lectures were published in the year they were presented, most after 1963 were published in the year following their presentation. Lectures for the missing years (above) and since 2006 were not published as books and are not listed.

2. In addition to the published John Dewey Lectures, at the request of John Dewey, the Society sponsored the publication of *The Use of Resources in Education* by Elsie Ripley Clapp (Harper, 1952)—a moving account of Elsie Ripley Clapp's work on developing people's resources in and through education in impoverished communities in rural Kentucky and West Virginia during the Great Depression. The Introduction to this book was written by John Dewey, in which he takes stock of the progressive education movement and the virulent attacks on the public schools.

PRESIDENTS OF THE JOHN DEWEY SOCIETY

One-Year Terms:

1935–1937	William Heard Kilpatrick (chairman)
1938–1957	William Heard Kilpatrick
1958–1961	H. Gordon Hullfish
1962–1963	George E. Axtelle

Two-Year Terms:

1964–1965	William Van Til
1966–1967	Joe R. Burnett
1968–1969	Glen Hass
1970–1971	Donald G. Arnstine
1972–1973	Jo Ann Boydston
1974–1975	Mary Anne Raywid
1976–1977	Vynce A. Hines
1978–1979	Louis Fischer
1980–1981	Richard Stephens
1982–1983	Arthur Brown
1984–1985	Glen Hass
1986–1987	Gerald Reagan
1988–1989	Arthur Wells Foshay
1990–1991	Jonas F. Soltis
1992–1993	William A. Schubert
1994–1995	Nel Noddings
1996–1997	Phillip W. Jackson
1998–1999	Elliot W. Eisner
2000–2001	Laurel Tanner
2002–2003	Daniel Tanner
2004–2005	David Hansen
2006–2007	Larry Hickman
2008–2009	James Garrison
2010–2011	Lynda Stone
2012–2013	Deron Boyles
2014–2015	Kathleen Knight Abovitz
2016–2017	A. G. Rud

A SOCIETY FOR THE STUDY OF EDUCATION
IN ITS SOCIAL RELATIONSHIPS*

Article 1: *Name*

(Name to be selected)

Article II: *Purposes*

The purpose of the society is to foster scholarly and scientific investigations of problems pertaining to the place and function of education in social change, and to publish the results of such studies.

Article III: *Membership*

Section 1.

a. Any person who is desirous of advancing the purposes of this organization is eligible for membership and may become a member upon payment of dues as prescribed.

b. There shall be two classes of members—members and fellows.

c. All members shall be entitled to vote as herein prescribed and to participate in discussion at meetings, but only fellows may be elected to the offices of the society.

Section 2.

Any member who has made a significant contribution to a yearbook or other investigation sponsored by the society shall, upon payment of dues as prescribed, become a fellow of the society. The executive board may elect as fellows others who have made significant contributions to the study of education in its social relationships.

---

*(Working draft of a Constitution presented at the Society's meeting on February 23, 1935)

Section 3.

Each yearbook shall contain the names of members and fellows.

Section 4.

The annual dues for members shall be $2.50. The entrance fee for members shall be $1.00. The annual dues for fellows shall be $3.50.

Article IV: *Officers*

Section 1.

The officers of the society shall consist of an executive board of seven, including the secretary. Six members of the board shall be elected by the members and fellows of the society for terms of three years each. The board shall elect from among its own members a president and from the fellows a secretary who shall thereupon become a member of the board, and such other officers as it may deem necessary.

Section 2.

a. The first executive board shall be elected at the meeting at which the society is organized. Two of the members of the board shall be elected for terms of three years, two for terms of two years, and two for terms of one year. Thereafter two members of the board shall be elected annually by ballot as hereinafter provided, and also members to fill out unexpired terms.

b. The annual election of members of the board shall be conducted by mail ballot. A primary election shall be held in March, in which fellows shall nominate from the list of fellows. The names of the six fellows receiving the highest number of votes on this primary ballot shall be submitted not later than the month of May to all members and fellows for a second ballot for the election of two members of the executive board. The two (or more, if unexpired terms are to be filled) receiving the highest vote in the May election shall be declared elected and take office July first. In the event that four vacancies are to be filled at any election, eight fellows shall be nominated in the primary election. The board shall prescribe all other necessary rules for elections.

Section 3.

The executive board shall have general charge of the work of the society; shall annually elect its own chairman; shall elect a secretary for a term of three years; shall fix the time and place of the meetings of the society; shall plan the program of research and publication and apportion the work; invite members who have rendered service to the society or its purposes to become fellows; appoint members to serve unexpired terms in the executive board until a successor shall be elected as provided in Section 2; and take such other actions are essential to the work of the society.

Article V: *Publications*

The society shall publish such materials as the executive board shall determine upon; but annually there shall be prepared and published a *yearbook.*

Article VI: *Amendments*

Proposals to amend this constitution may be made by the executive board or by a petition signed by fifty members. Such proposals shall be submitted to all members and fellows for a mail vote and shall be declared adopted if approved by two-thirds of the membership voting thereon.

Some Policies of the Society

1. *Period of Membership.* Applicants for membership may not date their entrance back of the current year, and all memberships terminate automatically on December 31st.

2. *Privileges of Membership.* In return for the annual dues of $2.50, regular members shall receive a doth-bound copy of each publication; are entitled to vote for the executive board and on amendments, and to participate in discussion in meetings of the society. In return for the annual dues of $3.50,

fellows shall receive a doth-bound copy of each publication; are entitled to vote for the executive board and on amendments, hold office, assist the executive board in policymaking and planning research and publications, and participate in discussions of the meetings.

3. *Payment of Dues.* Statement of dues shall be rendered in October and November for the following calendar year. Any member or fellow so notified whose dues remain unpaid on January first thereby loses his membership and can be reinstated as a regular member or fellow only by additional payment of the entrance fee of $1.00. Membership may not be held by institutions or libraries.

4. *Publications.* Publications, except those of the current year mailed to members, shall be for sale commercially. Whatever profits accrue from such sales shall go to increasing the scope of the work of the society.

5. *Secretary.* The secretary shall execute the orders of the executive board, of which he is a member. Records of membership, development of the programs, accounts, etc., shall be handled by him, subject to the policy set by the executive board.

There was a general discussion of the yearbook for the new society. The meeting was adjourned.

REFERENCES

Anderson, Archibald W. (1951). The task of educational theory. *Educational Theory*. 1 (May), 9–21.

Bayles, Ernest E. (1948). Is Mr. Hedges clear on education? in I. N. Thut (ed.), "By Way of Comment," *Educational Administration and Supervision*.34 (February), 114.

Board of Director of the American Education Fellowship. (1944–1945). Objectives and program of the American Education Fellowship. *Progressive Education*. 22 (1944–1945), 10.

Bode, Boyd H. (1935). Education and social reconstruction. *The Social Frontier*. 1 (January), 22.

Clapp, Elsie R. (1952). *The Use of Resources in Education*. New York: Harper & Row, Publishers.

Counts, George S. (1932). *Dare the School Build a New Social Order?* New York: John Day Company.

Counts, George S. (1971). A humble autobiography, Chapter five in Robert J. Havighurst (ed.), *Leaders in American Education*. Seventieth Yearbook of the National Society for the Study of Education, Part II. Chicago: University of Chicago Press.

Cremin, Lawrence A. (1961). The Transformation of the School, Progressivism in *American Education*. 1957–1976. New York: Alfred A. Knopf.

Cremin, Lawrence A. (1988). *American Education: The Metropolitan Experience, 1876–1980*. New York: Harper & Row, Publishers.

Cubberley, Ellwood P. (1947). *Public Education in the United States.* Boston: Houghton Mifflin Company.

Dewey, John (1899). The School and Society. Chicago: University of Chicago Press.

Dewey, John. (1916). *Democracy and Education.* New York: Macmillan Publishing Company.

Dewey, John. (1934). Education for a changing social order. *NEA Addresses and Proceedings.* 747–752.

Dewey, John. (1934). Can education share in social reconstruction? *The Social Frontier.* 1 (October), 11–12.

Dewey, John. (1939). *Education and Culture.* New York: G. P. Putnam's Sons.

Dykhuizen, George. (1973). *The Life and Mind of John Dewey.* Carbondale, Ill.: Southern Illinois University Press.

Engler, W. H. (1973). *Radical School Reforms of the 1960s.* Doctoral Dissertation. Rutgers University, New Brunswick, NJ.

Harap, Henry. (1970). The beginnings of the John Dewey Society. *Educational Theory.* 20 (Spring), 157–163.

Harris, Pickens E. (1939). The American school: A delinquent institution, Chapter 6 in Harold Rugg (ed.), *Democracy and the Curriculum.* New York: D. Appleton-Century Company.

Hedges, M. H. (1947). Major problems of education, in I. N. Thut (ed.), "By Way of Comment," *Educational Administration and Supervision.* 33 (December), 144.

Hook, Sidney. (1987). *Out of Step.* New York: Harper & Row, Publishers.

Hulburd, David. (1951). *This Happened in Pasadena.* New York: Macmillan.

Hullfish, H. Gordon (ed.). 1953. *Educational Freedom in an Age of Anxiety.* Twelfth Yearbook of the John Dewey Society. New York: Harper & Brothers.

Johnson, Henry C., Jr. (1977). Reflective thought and practical action: The origins of the John Dewey Society. *Educational Theory.* 27 (Winter), 65–75.

Kilpatrick, William H. (ed.). 1937. *The Teacher and Society.* First Yearbook of the John Dewey Society. New York: D. Appleton Century Company.

Meyer, Adolphe E. (1967). *An Educational History of the American People*, 2nd ed. New York: McGraw-Hill Book Company.

Myrdal, Gunnar. (1944). *An American Dilemma*. New York: Harper & Row.

Myrdal, Gunnar. (1969). *Objectivity in Social Research*. New York: Pantheon Books.

Newman, Robert E., Jr. (1960). *History of a Civic Education Project Implementing the Social-Problems Technique of Instruction*. Doctoral dissertation, Stanford University.

Nisbet, Robert (1980). *History of the Idea of Progress*. New York: Basic Books.

Ravitch, D. (1987). The Revisionists Revised. New York: Basic Books.

Rugg, Harold. (ed.). 1939. *Democracy and the Curriculum.*Third Yearbook of the John Dewey Society. New York: D. Appleton-Century Company.

Rugg, Harold. (1947). *Foundations for American Education.*Yonkers-on-Hudson, N.Y.: World Book Company.

Tanner, Daniel, & Tanner, Laurel (1990). *History of the School Curriculum*. New York: Macmillan.

Tanner, Daniel, & Tanner, Laurel (1997). *Curriculum Development: Theory into Practice*, 4th ed. Upper Saddle River, NJ: Pearson.

Tanner, Laurel (1997). *Dewey's Laboratory School: Lessons for Today*. New York: Teachers College Press.

Thut, I. N. (1946). By Way of Comment. *Educational Administration and Supervision*. 32 (November), 463–477.

Tyler, Ralph W. (1949). Basic Principles of Curriculum and Instruction. Chicago: University of Chicago Press.

Van Til, William. (1983). *My Way of Looking at It: An Autobiography*. Terre Haute, Ind.: Lake Lure Press.

ABOUT THE AUTHOR

Daniel Tanner is Professor Emeritus at the Graduate School of Education at Rutgers University where he established the doctoral program in curriculum studies. He previously served on the faculties of San Francisco State University, Purdue University, Northwestern University, City University of New York, and the University of Wisconsin-Milwaukee. He has lectured at the University of London (England), University of Kiel (Germany), University of Palacky (Czech Republic), Teachers College of Columbia University, University of Iowa, SUNY Buffalo, SUNY Binghamton, University of Delaware, Emory University, University of Missouri at Kansas City, and University of San Francisco.

Professor Tanner's major books include *Schools for Youth* (1965), *Secondary Curriculum: Theory and Development* (1971), *Secondary Education: Perspectives and Prospects* (1972), and with Laurel Tanner, *Curriculum Development: Theory into Practice* (1975, 1980, 1995, 2007), *Supervision in Education: Problems and Practices* (1987), and *History of the School Curriculum* (1990).

His writings have appeared in leading education journals, yearbooks of the National Society for the Study of Education (1988, 1990), The Atlantic Monthly, and The New York Times. One of his articles on the philosophy of John Dewey was published in *The Bulletin of the Atomic Scientists*. Among his many honors are the Distinguished Achievement Award in the Learned Article category from the Educational Press Association of America (1990); Lifetime Achievement Award, Curriculum Studies Division, American Educational Research Association (2006); Raywid Award, Society of Professors of Education (2008); and Distinguished Service Award, the John Dewey Society for the Study of Education and Culture (2010). He is a Fellow of the American Association for the Advancement of Science and Inaugural Fellow of the American Educational Research Association and has served on councils and committees of the Association for Supervision and Curriculum Development and the National Association of Secondary School Principals.

Professor Tanner holds the Ph.D. from The Ohio State University (1955), where he was named University Scholar. He was President of the John Dewey Society from 2002 through 2003.

NAME INDEX

SUBJECT INDEX